APIs: A Strategy Guide

Daniel Jacobson, Greg Brail, and Dan Woods

O'REILLY®

Beijing · Cambridge · Farnham · Köln · Sebastopol · Tokyo

APIs: A Strategy Guide

by Daniel Jacobson, Greg Brail, and Dan Woods

Published by O'Reilly Media, Inc., 1005 Gravenstein Highway North, Sebastopol, CA 95472.

O'Reilly books may be purchased for educational, business, or sales promotional use. Online editions are also available for most titles (*http://my.safaribooksonline.com*). For more information, contact our corporate/institutional sales department: (800) 998-9938 or *corporate@oreilly.com*.

Editor: Mary Treseler	**Cover Designer:** Karen Montgomery
Production Editor: Dan Fauxsmith	**Interior Designer:** David Futato
Proofreader: O'Reilly Production Services	**Illustrator:** Robert Romano

Revision History for the First Edition:

2011-12-14   First release

See *http://oreilly.com/catalog/errata.csp?isbn=9781449308926* for release details.

ISBN: 978-1-449-30892-6

[LSI]

1323816619

Table of Contents

Preface

Conventions Used in This Book

The following typographical conventions are used in this book:

Italic

> Indicates new terms, URLs, email addresses, filenames, and file extensions.

`Constant width`

> Used for program listings, as well as within paragraphs to refer to program elements such as variable or function names, databases, data types, environment variables, statements, and keywords.

`Constant width bold`

> Shows commands or other text that should be typed literally by the user.

`Constant width italic`

> Shows text that should be replaced with user-supplied values or by values determined by context.

 This icon signifies a tip, suggestion, or general note.

 This icon indicates a warning or caution.

Using Code Examples

This book is here to help you get your job done. In general, you may use the code in this book in your programs and documentation. You do not need to contact us for permission unless you're reproducing a significant portion of the code. For example, writing a program that uses several chunks of code from this book does not require permission. Selling or distributing a CD-ROM of examples from O'Reilly books does require permission. Answering a question by citing this book and quoting example code does not require permission. Incorporating a significant amount of example code from this book into your product's documentation does require permission.

We appreciate, but do not require, attribution. An attribution usually includes the title, author, publisher, and ISBN. For example: "*APIs: A Strategy Guide* by Daniel Jacobson, Greg Brail, and Dan Woods (O'Reilly). Copyright 2012 Evolved Media, 9781449308926."

If you feel your use of code examples falls outside fair use or the permission given above, feel free to contact us at *permissions@oreilly.com*.

Acknowledgments

This book would not have been possible without our unnamed author, Scott Regan. Scott was a tireless source of energy, leadership, and support. Scott was especially good at finding real-world examples that enliven the narrative.

John Musser contributed both content and tremendous insight from his broad work with APIs via the Programmable Web. He was a valuable sounding board and advisor about both big picture issues and details of technology.

Sam Ramji gave us his time and thought leadership in his interviews and reviews. Brian Mulloy also gave of his time and talents in this way. Harold Neal broke away from a busy schedule at the Center for American Progress to participate in interviews and reviews, and Shanley Kane gave us her insight on API community management. We particularly want to thank Chet Kapoor of Apigee for his perspective on the market and his support for the project.

We'd also like to thank the folks from the front lines of the API world who let us interview them, including Derek Willis and Derek Gottfrid, both of whom worked on The *New York Times'* API, Steve Smith and Chris Patti from AccuWeather, Tim Madewell from Innotas, Jason Sirota at XO Group Inc., and Kin Lane, the API evangelist himself. To all of you, your quotes bring this book to life and bring theory right down to the trenches of execution.

We would like to express our gratitude to Sophie Jasson-Holt, Deb Cameron, Dan Safarik, Deb Gabriel, and Henry Coupet from the Evolved Media team, all of whom provided the editorial and project management support that helped bring the book to life quickly and to a high degree of quality.

Daniel would also like to thank Michael Hart who started the Netflix API program and whose impact is implicitly referenced throughout this book in various Netflix examples. We'd also like to thank Zach Brand, who provided us with recent images and stats for NPR's API.

Although this book is largely drawn from our personal experiences in the API world, those experiences are enriched by our interactions with many great leaders in this space.

In particular, all of us have and continue to work with some of the brightest, most talented people in the industry, all of whom have influenced this book in subtle and not-so-subtle ways. Moreover, our perspectives have morphed over time due to some of the influential writings, presentations, informal conversations, and other interactions with myriad others who have pushed API innovation to where it is today. To all of these people (you know who you are), thank you for your indirect contributions and we look forward to seeing how this field develops moving forward.

Safari® Books Online

Safari Books Online is an on-demand digital library that lets you easily search over 7,500 technology and creative reference books and videos to find the answers you need quickly.

With a subscription, you can read any page and watch any video from our library online. Read books on your cell phone and mobile devices. Access new titles before they are available for print, and get exclusive access to manuscripts in development and post feedback for the authors. Copy and paste code samples, organize your favorites, download chapters, bookmark key sections, create notes, print out pages, and benefit from tons of other time-saving features.

O'Reilly Media has uploaded this book to the Safari Books Online service. To have full digital access to this book and others on similar topics from O'Reilly and other publishers, sign up for free at *http://my.safaribooksonline.com*.

How to Contact Us

Please address comments and questions concerning this book to the publisher:

> O'Reilly Media, Inc.
> 1005 Gravenstein Highway North
> Sebastopol, CA 95472
> 800-998-9938 (in the United States or Canada)
> 707-829-0515 (international or local)
> 707-829-0104 (fax)

We have a web page for this book, where we list errata, examples, and any additional information. You can access this page at:

> *http://www.oreilly.com/catalog/9781449308926*

To comment or ask technical questions about this book, send email to:

> *bookquestions@oreilly.com*

For more information about our books, courses, conferences, and news, see our website at *http://www.oreilly.com*.

Find us on Facebook: *http://facebook.com/oreilly*

Follow us on Twitter: *http://twitter.com/oreillymedia*

Watch us on YouTube: *http://www.youtube.com/oreillymedia*

CHAPTER 1

The API Opportunity

APIs are a big deal and they are getting bigger. Pioneering companies such as Google, Facebook, Apple, and Twitter have exposed amazing technological solutions to the public, transforming existing businesses and creating new industries. Central to these companies' successes are the APIs that link people and their computing devices to the underlying platforms that power each business and that tie these companies together behind the scenes.

The world is already changing. Consider the following examples:

- Salesforce.com built a large, rich partner ecosystem by opening core services for partners to innovate and extend. Today, more traffic comes through the Salesforce API than through its website. As of mid-2011 more than 60 percent of the traffic to Salesforce.com comes through APIs.

- Amazon opened its core computing infrastructure as Amazon Web Services (AWS), accessed via number of APIs, and now serves more bandwidth through AWS than through all of its global storefronts combined.

- Twitter is the most visible example of a business almost entirely based on an API and an ecosystem of developer applications.

- Netflix has completely reinvented how we consume movies and TV shows with streaming to hundreds of different devices, upending not just the video rental industry but also impacting large adjacent markets such as cable TV. APIs allow Netflix to support a multitude of devices in an affordable manner.

- NPR has infused its API into the engineering culture of the digital media division. The API drives the website, mobile apps, and all other forms of distribution and syndication for the company. The API has also transformed the company's relationship with its member stations and the way that NPR shares content with them.

Now consider these industry trends:

- Smartphone sales passed new PC sales in early 2011, and Morgan Stanley predicts that by the end of 2012, there will be more connected mobile devices in the world than PCs.

- CTIA (the wireless industry association) has determined that there are already more wireless devices in the United States than people.

- Analysts are competing to predict how many mobile devices will exist in the future. The GSMA (another wireless industry association) predicts that there will be 20 billion connected mobile devices by 2020, and Ericsson CEO Hans Vestberg predicts 50 billion. Meanwhile, Marthin De Beer, Senior Vice President of Cisco's Emerging Technologies Group, projects that count to be over a trillion by 2020.

- Cisco predicts that while Internet traffic originated by PCs will continue to grow at 33 percent per year, traffic originated by non-PC devices will more than double each year by 2015.

- Facebook accounts for over 25 percent of total Internet page views at this writing, and APIs drive both the Facebook products and its ecosystem.

- Over 30 percent of Internet traffic during US prime-time hours comes from Netflix streaming, which is delivered and managed via APIs.

These statistics point not only to an explosion of overall Internet traffic, but also to a huge shift in the distribution of this traffic towards apps and devices. Looking at these accelerating trends, it's very easy to imagine that APIs will likely power most of your Internet traffic within a few years.

Why We Wrote This Book

As authors, we are coming at this topic fresh from our experiences in the trenches. Daniel Jacobson led development of the NPR content management system and the API that draws from that system. The NPR API is now the centerpiece of NPR's digital distribution strategy, transforming NPR's ability to reach its audience on a wide range of platforms.

Today, Daniel leads the development of APIs at Netflix, whose API strategy is in the critical path of the Netflix streaming service. Netflix's ability to provide rich video experiences on hundreds of devices is powered by this service and has dramatically increased the rate at which new implementations can be built and delivered to new devices. Through this program, Netflix's user base has grown tremendously, resulting in API growth from under one billion requests per month to more than one billion requests per day, in one year.

Greg Brail writes based on his work as CTO of Apigee, where he has helped implement dozens of API programs and been exposed to many more. In this role he is also able to draw from the collective wisdom of the Apigee team, who has met hundreds of developers and also learned from hundreds of enterprise API programs.

We wrote this book to help people understand the potential of APIs. Additionally, we want you to go into creating an API with your eyes wide open. This book is not a programming manual but a best practices manual. You need to understand both the opportunity and the tactical issues related to creating an API.

This book will also introduce business executives and technologists to the land of API opportunity. To be sure, the world of APIs involves lots of technology, but what often gets lost in the shuffle is the business impact of APIs. This book is about how to think about APIs from a business perspective and how APIs can have a positive impact on your business.

We also want to educate you on what you're getting yourself into when you decide to develop an API. What are the implications of offering an API, not just from a technology standpoint but also in terms of business strategy, legal and rights considerations, and relationships with partners?

What we are going to demonstrate is that APIs are having a profound impact on the world of business—and that the time to act is now.

Unlike many other discussions of APIs that exclusively look at the way that large Internet-based companies use APIs publicly, this book also emphasizes the private use of APIs, which we believe has an even greater impact than many of the more prolific public API programs you often read about.

As authors, we must keep one foot in the world of technology and one foot in the world of business. To that end, we hope to educate creative executives and technologists about how to put APIs to work in the context of their own businesses.

In this book, we'll talk about:

- The business opportunity for APIs
- Examples of companies using APIs to transform their business and in some cases their industries
- Business models being used for APIs
- What an API value chain looks like and how to enable the different pieces of that value chain
- Considerations for crafting your API strategy and responding to concerns and objections
- Issues around API design, especially how to make adoption easy for developers
- What to do about API security, including coverage of OAuth
- The legal implications of running an API business, including privacy and data rights
- Considerations for operating your API at scale
- How to think about metrics and measuring your API program
- Engaging developers and building community to drive adoption of your API

In summary, this book offers a roadmap for using APIs to transform your business.

Who Is This Book For?

There are a range of books on the technical aspects of APIs, including books about REST, OAuth, XML, JSON, and others. This book is not intended to compete with those books. In fact, although it is virtually impossible to address APIs without delving into technical approaches, this book is not targeted at the technologists who build or directly consume APIs. Rather, this book is designed for the people who need to make the strategic decisions about whether an API is a good idea for their company.

Target audiences for this book include C-level executives, members of the business development teams, product managers, and technical evangelists. Of course, there will be plenty in this book for technologists as well, but at a higher level.

What Is an API?

API stands for application programming interface. An API can provide a hook for colleagues, partners, or third-party developers to access data and services to build applications such as iPhone apps quickly. The Twitter and Facebook APIs are famous examples. There are APIs that are open to any developer, APIs that are open only to partners, and APIs that are used internally to help run the business better and facilitate collaboration between teams.

An API, then, is essentially a contract. Once such a contract is in place, developers are enticed to use the API because they know they can rely on it. The contract increases confidence, which increases use. The contract also makes the connection between provider and consumer much more efficient since the interfaces are documented, consistent, and predictable.

How Is an API Different from a Website?

An API is quite different from a website. A website provides information on demand. A company puts content out in the world, and people consume it. Websites have no contracts or structures around the use of content. If content on the website changes, visitors who come next get the new content. Their browsers are not affected, and any change is transparent to the user. If you dramatically redesign the website, the only impact is on the user accustomed to seeing the content laid out in a particular way. Humans are great at visual pattern matching; we can quickly adjust to a new design and find what we need. That doesn't mean that users don't complain when their favorite site is redesigned, but they almost always adapt.

An API is quite different because it has a contract, and programs are built on top of that contract. Programs, unlike humans, are not flexible and almost always terrible at pattern matching. If you alter anything in the contract of the API, the ripple effect on the apps built on top of it is potentially quite large.

Our Working Definition of an API

Technical definition: An API is a way for two computer applications to talk to each other over a network (predominantly the Internet) using a common language that they both understand.

APIs follow a specification, meaning:

- The API provider describes exactly what functionality the API will offer
- The API provider describes when the functionality will be available and when it might change in an incompatible way
- The API provider may outline additional technical constraints within the API, such as rate limits that control how many times a particular application or end user is allowed to use the API in a given hour, day, or month
- The API provider may outline additional legal or business constraints when using the API, such as branding limitations, types of use, and so on
- Developers agree to use the API as described, to use only the APIs that are described, and to follow the rules set out by the API provider

In addition, the API provider may offer other tools, such as:

- Mechanisms to access the API and understand its terms of use
- Documentation to aid in understanding the API
- Resources such as example programs and developer communities to support those using the API
- Operational information about the health of the API and how much use it is getting

 Remember that the structure of the API is part of the contract. The contract is binding, and it cannot be changed casually.

You should treat an API like a software product, taking into account versioning, backward compatibility, and ramp-up time to accommodate any new functionality. There should be a balance between supporting your existing base while at the same time keeping up with necessary changes so that your API grows with your business and follows its planned evolution.

This does not mean that the API can never change. On the contrary, an API is an online product that can change almost constantly to meet the needs of the business, or to serve the current traffic load in the most efficient way. But these are changes to the implementation, not to the interface. When done right, the implementation of an API can change on a daily basis, or even more often, while the interface remains consistent.

...But APIs and Websites Have a Lot in Common

APIs, like websites, are expected to be available 24/7, 365 days a year. Developers, like website users, do not have much patience for "scheduled downtime" every Saturday morning. All of this can create a challenge for building an API on an existing enterprise technology infrastructure, using systems that may have been designed with an "end of day" cycle, after which they are shut down until the next day (such as banking systems).

Successful websites can, and are, updated continuously to change the design and tweak features. This is possible because websites are live entities out on the network that can be easily changed without changing the clients—there is no need to push a software update to the users.

APIs are not much different in this respect. Assuming your API remains backward compatible, an API program can introduce new features and change the implementation of existing features without "breaking" the clients. As long as you uphold the contract between your API and the developers who use it, the API can change on a "web schedule" rather than on an "enterprise IT schedule." The result is a better, more responsive API program.

In fact, changes to both APIs and websites can be driven by analytics on behavior of the applications and end users. In both cases, a good design and product management team constantly checks the analytics to see what parts of the site or API are succeeding and which are failing. The result should feed into regular development sprints, which over time build a much more robust API or website.

Who Uses an API?

We call the company or organization that offers an API the *API provider*. This book is largely aimed at API providers (or those who are thinking about offering an API).

We decided to call the people who use your API to create applications *developers*. It's true that many types of people may be interested in your API, including business owners, marketing gurus, executives, and others, but the people who will eventually create the applications are developers. Developers are the primary audience for your API.

We decided to call the people who use the applications that developers create *end users*. They are the secondary audience for your API and often the audience driving many of your API decisions. Depending on the content made available via your API, you may have particular concerns to address, such as copyright, legal use, and so on, that relate to this secondary audience.

Types of APIs

We see two types of APIs: private and public. No matter what you may hear in the media, private APIs are the more prevalent variety. You know about the Facebooks and Twitters of the world and their use of APIs. What you probably don't know is that those same companies are likely making much more extensive use of their own APIs to drive their websites, mobile apps, and other customer-facing products. In our experience, visible public APIs like these are just the tip of the iceberg. Like the large underwater mass of an iceberg, most APIs are private and imperceptible, internal to companies, used by staff and by partners with contractual agreements. This use of APIs is what is really driving the API revolution. Do not limit your thinking about the ways APIs can be used to public examples like the App Store. Partner and internal use of APIs is often more valuable.

Much of the discussion of APIs assumes that they must be open to the public to be of value. This is not the case. We believe that private APIs are having a transformational impact on most companies, in many cases much more so than public APIs.

The *New York Times* API started as a private API and is transforming their business. "The NYT API grew out of a need to make our own internal content management system more accessible so that we could get the most from our content," said Derek Willis, Newsroom Developer at the *Times*. "The API offered a way to give more people access to create more interesting pieces. We are the biggest users of our own API, and that's not by accident. The API helps our business in other ways: creating brand awareness and helping us attract talent. But fundamentally, it helps us do our own jobs better."

To further frame this discussion, let's clarify what we mean by public and private. Public means that the API is available to almost anyone with little or no contractual arrangement (beyond agreement to the terms of use) with the API provider. Private APIs are used in a variety of ways, whether to support internal API efforts or a partner's use of the API. API providers also offer private APIs to large customers with appropriate legal contracts. Private and public really refers to the formality of the business arrangement. It doesn't refer to the API content nor does it refer to the applications developed using the API.

Finally, public and private APIs are, in the end, still APIs. Often a company will start with a private API and eventually open some or all of it for public access, possibly with additional restrictions. Other times, a company will launch a public API, then realize how important it is for internal development and in the end it is private use, not public use, that provides the real business benefit.

AccuWeather, for example, is well known for providing weather data to the general public, which would lead most to believe that their APIs are public. But remember: the private/public distinction refers to the arrangement with partners, not to the availability of content to end-users. AccuWeather's API, like other private APIs, can be and is used to offer applications to the general public.

AccuWeather's API is highly customized for partners; it's a key differentiator. "We have over 300 variations of our API. This is a result of our company philosophy—custom for the customer, or for each company using the API," said Chris Patti, director of technology at AccuWeather. "We respond on a dime to customer requests, and it's a competitive advantage for us. We've won contracts by being able to respond to custom requests, like serving data vs. GPS coordinates. This is why customers work with us, because of our creativity and responsiveness."

API providers often choose to offer different views of business assets internally and externally. Derek Willis said, "We might offer more than one version of an API to support multiple use cases or business models. We might have different API endpoints for different audiences. For example, the public article search may offer only truncated articles while the internal article search API might offer the full text."

Why Now?

APIs have reached their breakout moment for three reasons:

Process maturity
   APIs are not just about technology. As in many business problems, what we really have is a people problem. APIs offer a common pattern to help people to collaborate.

Self-service
   Why did open source succeed? Although the availability of source code is often the focus of discussions about the success of open source, the idea of self-service is much more important. Only a tiny percentage of developers wanted to read or modify source code. Instead, open source software displaced commercial software because developers did not have to ask anyone for permission to take the software and run with it. Publishers of APIs learned from open source. A successful API must be available on a self-service basis and be easy to use. Like open source projects, the best APIs have thriving online communities, either internal to the company or in the larger public developer community (or both). In the most successful developer communities, the most active members don't work for the company that provides the API—rather, they help because the API is critical to what they do and they love helping others see its value.

Technological maturity
   Even though technologists have used APIs for decades, few people realize that the explosion of activity going on with Twitter, Netflix, and others online is based on APIs. The end result that people see is a lot of traffic, but it's not web traffic. It's API traffic. Companies like Google, Amazon, Twitter, Sears, Alcatel-Lucent, and thousands of others are using APIs to change their businesses.

In brief, tech blogger Robert Scoble summed up where we are now by defining three eras:

- Web 1994 was the "get me a domain and a page" era
- Web 2000 was the "make my pages interactive and put people on it" era
- Web 2010 is the "get rid of pages and glue APIs and people together" era

We believe that this profound shift will continue and that it's important for you to know more about it. Chapter 2 describes the impetus behind APIs as a business strategy.

APIs as a Business Strategy

If you live in the world of technology, you probably don't need much convincing that APIs are an important trend with significant business impact. But if you are not immersed in the world of technology, it may not be as obvious why APIs matter to your business.

APIs are breaking out into more and more business arenas every day. The arguments we present in this chapter should help demonstrate to those outside the world of technology the importance of APIs. We also intend to offer a script for prime influencers that must convince others about the value of adopting an API strategy.

Today, we are seeing an explosion in consumption models. Why? Largely because of apps and mobile devices. We are rapidly moving from about a billion laptops with web browsers to as many as a trillion connected devices with apps by 2020, if we go by De Beer's estimate. Most companies are seeing their customers move quickly beyond browser-based web apps. If you want to continue to be successful—or even stay in business—you need to be where your customers are!

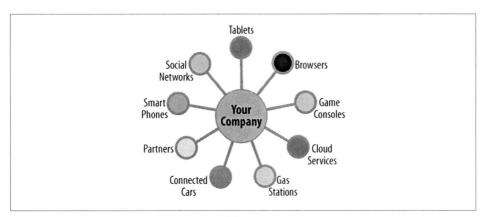

Figure 2-1. The explosion of consumption models

Additionally, the pace of change is faster than ever. Markets are changing so fast that you can't spend enough time to calculate market size, conduct focus groups, plan, develop, launch because by the time you do, the market niche may be gone or fundamentally changed.

 Your customers are quickly moving from a browser-based model to a model of consumption that involves consuming your services through apps on mobile devices.

End users use a large number of different connected device types, social networks, and various forms of messaging to access the information and services they need. They often move from one way of using a company's services to another, and they expect their applications to keep up with them as they move. For example, it is not at all uncommon for someone to start watching a movie streamed by Netflix using a WiFi-enabled TV but finish it on a different device, such as their iPhone, while waiting at the doctor's office.

The same is true for reading a book. The bookmarks and comments that you store on your Amazon Kindle also show up when you read the same book using the Kindle iPad app, or the Kindle app on your computer. You can buy a book on the Amazon Android app and then read it on your computer. And if you start reading on one device, when you load the same book on a different device, Kindle can open the book on the page that you were on when reading on the first device.

What's probably behind all of these app experiences? Behind most of these great apps is a great API. APIs can be thought of as the "backend" of an app, enabling the app to reach into a company's data or services. APIs are key to enabling a rich app ecosystem that extends customer reach.

Although all of these experiences could be possible without APIs, the pervasiveness and the rate at which companies with strong APIs are progressing would not be possible. APIs make it relatively easy for companies to scale up dozens or hundreds of implementations in a relatively short period of time. Some of these scenarios were difficult to support at first, but they are getting much easier. Practices for successfully using APIs are slowly emerging, and technology infrastructure to support them is maturing. Market conditions have changed in ways that make APIs relevant to any business with assets that others would like to use. It is not just the largest companies in the world or the hottest startups that can benefit from APIs.

For example, Sears provided its massive product catalog, perhaps the deepest and most complete catalog in the world, for developers to place on their websites or in apps. In doing so, they've been able to increase distribution and sales.

The World Bank offers data for developers to use and create apps that can create further awareness of global economic development issues, providing new ways for people to explore the data. StatPlanet is one example of an application built using this API, which offers interactive maps, graphs, and timelines (see Figure 2-2).

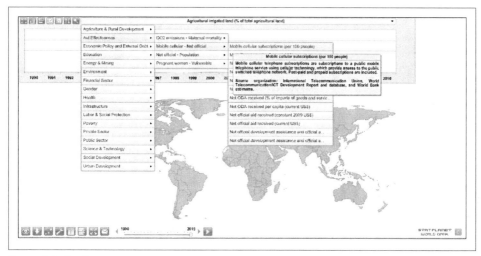

Figure 2-2. StatPlanet

Even Proctor and Gamble has gotten into the app game, having its signature toilet paper brand, Charmin, sponsor an infamous app for finding public toilets. Now there's a creative way to promote brand loyalty!

The Growth of APIs

Evidence of the growth of activity related to APIs can be tracked by looking at public APIs. This is simply because private APIs are, well, private, and therefore more difficult to track. ProgrammableWeb.com tracks the creation of publicly accessible APIs. The accelerating growth of such APIs is shown in Figure 2-3.

Figure 2-3 represents just a fraction of the APIs out there. ProgrammableWeb does not track many kinds of APIs, which, if included, would increase the total number of APIs by a substantial margin, perhaps even exponentially. Most of the generalizable statistics we have come from the world of public APIs, but our experience indicates that private APIs are enjoying a similar burst in growth. Moreover, we believe that private APIs are already substantially more important to most companies than public APIs.

A look at popular consumer and business services shows how APIs have become the primary conduit for traffic. Sites like Twitter, Google, Netflix, eBay, Salesforce.com, and others now get more than half of their traffic through APIs. Consider the following statistics:

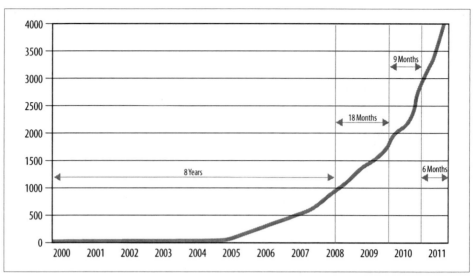

Figure 2-3. Accelerating growth in public APIs (source: ProgrammableWeb)

- Twitter: More than 15 billion calls per day as of July 2011, with 75 percent of traffic coming through the API
- Netflix: More than 1 billion calls per day as of October 2011
- Amazon Web Services: More than 260 billion objects stored in S3 as of January 2011
- NPR: 3.2 billion stories delivered via the API per month as of October 2011
- Google: 5 billion calls per day
- Facebook: 5 billion calls per day

In the face of this sort of evidence, clearly APIs are becoming a conduit for a tremendous volume of communication and commerce. As with many technology trends, the first movers are technology-savvy startups. They are being followed by a whole raft of newer arrivals to this space who have started building API-based channels. Such companies include financial services firms like TradeKing, media companies like NPR, The *New York Times*, *USA Today*, *Financial Times*, and The *Guardian*, retailers like Best Buy, Tesco, Sears, and Amazon, and automotive companies like Ford and General Motors.

The use of APIs by companies who do not make their use widely known is also increasing. Many companies are reinventing the way applications are built within their own enterprises by exposing their existing assets as APIs, enabling their internal developers to build innovative new mobile, social, and cloud apps. Many of what you may think of as "traditional enterprises" are employing APIs to increase their overall agility in delivering applications and to open up new opportunities for dealing with partners.

APIs are exploding, and the number of APIs you don't know about far surpasses the number of APIs you do know about.

Why You Might Need an API

How do you know whether you might benefit from having an API? Here we present some common triggers that have inspired companies to create an API.

You Need a Second Mobile App

When companies realize they need a mobile application, time is typically of the essence. The first mobile application is usually created quickly in response to a pressing need and written to run on at least one of the most popular platforms at the time (right now, iOS and Android). This sometimes results in leveraging existing technologies, like extending RSS (Really Simple Syndication) feeds, to meet the short-term targets. When it comes time to create a second mobile application, however, it dawns on the company that they are at risk of repeating a great deal of work. When that happens, they begin to look for ways to make mobile application creation more efficient. How could other devices leverage the same system? Are there any repeatable components? Might providing a private API encourage others external to the service tier of your company to do some of this work?

If your mobile app strategy is a success, you will need apps that run on iOS and Android. And then it might need to run on Windows Phone. Then don't forget about RIM. And then all of the emerging tablet devices. The point is that, depending on your company's strategy, mobile applications may need to run on two, three, or even more platforms.

The creation of mobile apps to support a variety of devices often leads to a discussion about creating an API. An API can help companies support multiple devices.

Your Customers or Partners Ask for an API

Sometimes sophisticated customers or partners ask if you have an API to help make a technical integration easier. For example, Silverpop, an email marketing company, found that once the largest companies in the world started using its product, the companies wanted tight integration of email marketing capabilities and other marketing automation applications. The obvious solution for this integration was an API.

Getty Images, a photo-licensing firm, had customers who wanted to bypass the firm's website and integrate photos for licensing in their publishing and production applications. The obvious solution here was also an API.

APIs improve on older technologies for interacting with customers. File transfer, EDI, IBM MQSeries channels and the like are all much more cumbersome ways to interact directly with customers' systems than a modern API.

AccuWeather never anticipated what would happen when one partner asked for an API. "The AccuWeather API started really without full architecture review and planning. We viewed it as a one-off request," admitted Chris Patti, Director of Technology. "We had a request from a major handset manufacturer for a widget to expose another data feed via HTTP. We put a junior developer on it. Then we saw demand for more types of data—radar and imagery." It didn't take long before it picked up steam. "Next thing we knew—every customer wanted it. We couldn't have imagined what it turned into. This wasn't a line of business—it just showed up. We knew we needed to react fast and plan, but time was not on our side."

Your Site Is Getting Screen-Scraped

If your site is getting screen-scraped, this could be considered a sort of passive-aggressive request for a public API. You obviously have business assets that developers would like to access. Offering an API lets you exert control over your data and the terms of its use. The best way to determine your next steps is to talk to the people doing the screen scraping to see what they are trying to do.

You Need More Flexibility in Providing Content

The ultimate reason for offering an API is to provide content or services in a flexible way. Originally, that's what websites were for (and they still are). When companies first looked for new ways to distribute their content beyond the website, many turned to methods like RSS feeds. For a variety of reasons, neither websites nor RSS feeds are enough to handle the flexibility most companies need these days. APIs can provide the ultimate level of flexibility for providing content when and how you want to, under your terms and with better control, while meeting your users' needs.

You Have Data to Make Available

It is quite common for companies or government organizations to have treasure troves of data that they have no time to make use of. For example, the Metropolitan Transit Authority (MTA) in New York City has information about the schedules, routes, and operational status of the subways. Instead of keeping this information under lock and key, the MTA created files in Google Transit format so that Google developers can use this information to create applications. Dozens of applications were created using the data. The Federal Aviation Administration (FAA) has done the same thing with data about commercial flights.

The same model works inside companies when a department has an important database that it does not have time to use. A private API can allow other departments to benefit from the data.

Data distribution is an important API function for content providers. For example, NPR allows member stations to write their own content into a private writable area of the NPR API. A particularly compelling use-case is Northwest News Network (N3), a network of 11 radio stations in Washington, Oregon, and Idaho. N3 creates stories and aggregates stories from the other 11 stations in an effort to act as a redistribution channel for the entire N3 network. N3's solution is to compile the stories for the network and write them into the NPR API. From there, each of the 11 stations can access individual stories, stories from a particular N3 station, or stories from the entire network through the NPR API to present the N3 content on their own sites and apps.

Your Competition Has an API

When one company in an industry publishes a public API, it is quite common for the rest of the industry to follow suit. In a way, this is a more general case of a customer requesting an API from a particular company. In this case, all of the end users in a market are in effect requesting an API from an industry. Certain clusters like retail, video, media, and social networking are effectively in an arms race with respect to their APIs. They are constantly trying to improve them and outdo the competition.

You Want to Let Potential Partners Test the Waters

When a potential partner wants to do business with a company, the company can steer them to an API that allows the partnership to get started. By adjusting the terms of the API properly, it is possible to let potential partners start experimenting with the API and converting to a more formal partnership when the partnership starts to generate enough mutually beneficial revenue or traffic. An API removes barriers to experimentation.

You Want to Scale Integration with Customers and Partners

Having an API provides a simpler and more flexible way to integrate with high-volume customers and partners. Customers who have their choice of vendors are attracted to companies that are set up to succeed quickly. An API sends the message that you are in such a position.

Traditionally, industries have created complex and proprietary ways to integrate. The financial services industry, for instance, created a large and complex network of technologies and services, including such successes as the SWIFT consortium, the FIX protocol, and the FpML standard. The travel industry created the largest-scale transaction processing systems of their time through reservation platforms such as SABRE. Other industries banded together to create further standards such as EDI, and still others relied on file transfers, emails, faxes, and computer tapes sent via FedEx.

Today, API technology—HTTP, REST, and JSON—is significantly simpler than all those options, pre-built for the Internet, and understood by a growing community of software professionals. A company looking for a way to connect to high-volume customers or an industry organization looking for a new way to connect its members would need a very good reason to choose any other option.

The Origin of the Innotas API

Innotas provides cloud solutions for IT management. We spoke with Tim Madewell about how the company decided to offer an API.

Why did Innotas decide to offer an API?

We had a compelling event—a customer needed it.

In the early days of our company, our average customer size was 25-30 users, but as our deal size grew and the SaaS market became more mature and accepted as an enterprise software solution, we started working with larger enterprise customers and the product needed to expand to meet the needs of an enterprise architecture as opposed to being a standalone tool.

So when we landed our first 5000-user account, we found that one of many requirements was that we enable integration from their backend CRM, HR, and billing system.

The API enabled us to offer this integration in a way that is standards-based so that it can be consumed by many customers and was flexible enough to be used by customers in many ways. We took a coarse-grained approach by building the API on a standard model that first offered our major data entities supporting backend enterprise systems such as CRM, HR, and Financials. We continued to release updates to our API with each product release that exposed additional data entities. One important distinction we made early on was to leave the business processes and business transaction logic outside the API and in the hands of the customer. Instead, we provided access and exposed the building blocks (data entities) for our customers to design and implement application-specific business transactions.

The API enabled us to offer this integration in a way that many customers could use it. We built the API on a standard model that first offered our major data entities.

Exposing the API where the customers can "come and get it" worked well for large customers. They have the resources to take the API and run with it to make the integration happen.

In hindsight, offering an API for integration was a good decision early on. It gave our customers a lot more flexibility in deciding what to do and gave Innotas the opportunity to be part of the customers' enterprise solution architecture.

An API Improves the Technical Architecture

Sometimes, building an API will simply improve the system's architecture for technical reasons, as opposed to business reasons. The NPR API was originally built for this reason. In 2007, NPR's digital properties were all served by a single Oracle database, which represented a single point of failure. The systems team needed to migrate this database to a MySQL cluster to allow for redundancy and scalability. But at the time, the NPR website, the CMS, and the database were too tightly bound to each other. The solution was to build an API between the website and the database. Once the API was built and the website was refactored to draw from it, the work to swap out the Oracle database for the MySQL cluster was substantially easier. Creating a separation layer between the systems allowed much more flexibility for the migration.

There are many, many more reasons for offering an API. The main point is: listen to your partners. Listen to your customers. Listen to your internal developers. See the way the industry is going. Consider how you might want to go there as well.

CHAPTER 3

Understanding the API Value Chain

Browser-based web apps represent a direct channel right from you to the consumer; consumers buy goods or services directly from you via your website. It's important to recognize that APIs represent an indirect channel for working with channel partners (developers) to reach end users.

To really understand what we mean by an indirect channel, we need to look at an example of a direct channel. In the early 1900s, people in the New York City garment district sold clothes right from the same building where they made the clothes. That's a direct channel. As the population moved to the suburbs in the 50s and 60s, retailers such as Sears, Montgomery Ward, and Macy's started selling a manufacturer's clothes as channel partners to provide distribution through an indirect channel, through channel partners.

The point here is that offering an API is not just a technology problem; it's a people and process problem as well. This chapter describes the anatomy of this channel so that you can understand all the players and all the different pressure points.

As always in this book, we're not just going to talk about public APIs; we're also going to talk about private APIs that you might offer to employees, customers, or partners.

Defining the Value Chain: Ask Key Questions

In order to understand what is happening when an API is being used to advance a business, it helps to ask the following questions:

- Who is the API provider? How will the API be published and promoted? Are the owner of the business assets and the API provider members of the same organization? For example, a mapping provider like Yahoo! may license mapping data from another provider.

- Who is the target audience for the API? What is the size of that audience? What is their motivation to consume the API? How will they benefit from it? For example, the API may target mobile app developers building location-based applications.

- What business assets are going to be provided through the API? What information, services, and products will be available? Of what potential value could these assets be to others? How will the owner of the business assets benefit from the API? For a mapping API, the assets are the mapping data and the points of interest.
- What types of apps will the API support? What features and functions will these apps have? For example, mobile apps on the iOS and Android platforms may provide GPS functionality that can be used to get the most out of mapping data.
- Who will use the apps created using the API? What benefit will they gain from using the apps? What benefits will the developers, the API provider, and the owner of the business assets get from their use? In our example, using the app, end users can perform local searches wherever they are.

The answers to these questions give us the elements of the API value chain. Figure 3-1 demonstrates the process by which you transform business assets into value for the end user through this indirect API channel.

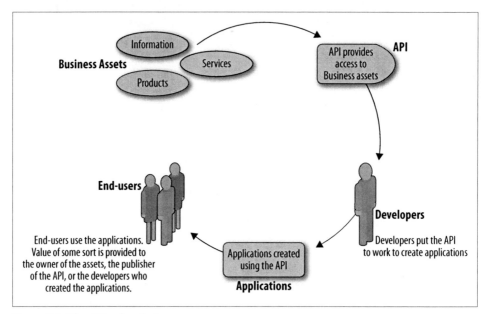

Figure 3-1. The API value chain

A closer look at Figure 3-1 allows us to uncover the motivations of everyone involved in bringing an API to life as a way to help a business execute its strategy.

The value chain starts with *business assets*, something that a business wants to allow others to use. Business assets can range from a product catalog to geospatial maps to Twitter posts to airline status information to services that allow products in the physical world to be controlled by virtual services such as payment systems. If there is nothing of value in the business assets, the API won't succeed. As we will see in later discussions of strategy, one common mistake is not confirming that the assets you are exposing through your API have value to the end users you are trying to reach. In addition, it is vital to understand how exposing the business assets will eventually benefit the owner of the business assets.

The next step is to create an API to expose those business assets. The API *provider's* job is to design the API so that the intended audiences can make the best use of it. Most of the time the provider is the same as the owner of the business assets, but not always. If they are the same organization, then the benefits simply flow back to the business owner. However, if the provider is a different organization, the provider usually needs to establish an agreement for redistribution to reward both the owner of the business assets and the API provider.

Once the API is published, some population of *developers* will hopefully put the API to use to create apps. As you might remember from the Introduction, we use this term in the broadest sense possible; it can include product managers who lead teams of developers or business analysts or executives interested in APIs as well as individual developers.

Once created, the *application* must then find its way into the hands of users. This means that the app must somehow be discoverable and obtainable by the intended user population. Some API providers offer app stores or other distribution and marketing assistance for this purpose. But in order to have value to a business, the apps created by the developers must be able to find their way into the hands of end users.

Finally, *end users* will hopefully use the apps in some way that they benefit from but also provide value to the owner of the business assets, the provider, and the developer.

When API strategies fail, it is often because one or more of the links in this value chain are too weak to support the creation of a healthy API economy.

One key is getting stakeholders from across the business involved in your API strategy. "Don't make an API program just an IT or developer initiative," says Kin Lane, developer evangelist at Mimeo. "You need to get other departments involved. On their own, the API team's developers might make some wrong assumptions—they are too close to it."

Bring multiple disciplines to the API when you are launching it. Get everyone at the table. If it's not meeting the core business objectives, if it doesn't speak to the outside world, and if the average person can't understand the purpose—chances are the program will get in trouble," advises Lane.

Creating a Private API Value Chain

The value proposition of public and private APIs will vary depending on the nature of the business. To understand this point completely, first we must explain how private APIs are used.

For example, leading companies see that apps can be built quickly using platforms like Amazon Elastic Compute Cloud (EC2) and Facebook. As a result, some of these companies are radically changing their own approach to app development. Some of them are exposing their business assets to internal developers who use APIs while also switching to a cloud-based infrastructure to accelerate their rate of innovation and development for these apps. In the process, they are also attracting young talent who are used to building apps quickly in this way.

Here are the elements of a private API value chain:

The business assets
> In private APIs, a company may have no interest or right in having these business assets used outside of their organization or outside of a tightly controlled domain. The apps created by private use of APIs may or may not be used in public. For example, a company might want to make operational data more easily available to decision makers, or might want to reach a partner's customer base.

The API provider
> The API provider is often the same party as the owner of the business assets. A private API is private because it is available only to an authorized population of developers. Within a company, this might be a specific group or IT.

Developers
> Developers using a private API are often employees of the organization that owns the business assets and publishes the API or partners with a close relationship with the business. Developers within a company might be other employees within other development groups or developers within a known business partner.

Applications
> The apps created by a private API can be used internally, by partners, publicly, or all of the above. Depending on the way that the apps are going to be used, attention to promotion and distribution varies widely.

Ways to Use a Private API

Private APIs can be applied in a variety of ways:

- Private APIs can be used to create apps to release to the public. This model is often used by large brands with the resources to develop apps and who want to control what their public apps do. After all, who knows your brand, your content, and your service offering better than you do?

- Private APIs can be used by partners to create apps or to implement integration services. Many SaaS companies offer this type of API. Think of software companies that offer integration services with Salesforce

- Private APIs can be used as a way to more efficiently build apps for internal use in an organization. For example, a large manufacturing company uses APIs to enable developers to build executive dashboards for distribution on tablet devices instead of requiring developers to request access to backend systems directly

Let's take a closer look at each of these.

Efficiently Creating Public Apps

In our experience, the biggest and most far-reaching impact of many private APIs is when companies use their API internally to build public apps. Using an API in this way tremendously increases efficiencies in extending products or features for customers. At a time when many companies are struggling to produce iPhone apps, companies with APIs have already released multiple versions of iPhone, Android, iPad, and other mobile apps.

An example of a private API used in this way is the NPR API and the NPR News iPhone app. NPR maintains a public API, but they also use a private API with greater rights and functionality to enable the development of various mobile apps. The iPhone apps were actually built by an external company called Bottle Rocket, a company that specializes in iPhone app development. NPR, at the time, did not have the skills in house to build the app, but the app is now owned by NPR. In fact, NPR largely designed it as well. Internal NPR staff also managed the project. But Bottle Rocket actually built the Objective-C code. The bridge between the two companies' work is the private API, which enabled Bottle Rocket's code to access NPR's content in a very powerful and scalable way.

Supporting Partner Relationships

Private APIs can be used to create apps that support partner relationships. This model works extremely well when a partner has a business reason to use the API to create an app but lacks the technology skills to create the apps. The owner of the business assets or the provider of the API can arrange for developers to create the app so that the partner can put it to use.

Apps created by internal teams to support partners include the use of private APIs to support channel relationships. Large retailers are using APIs to allow thousands of companies participating in cooperative marketing programs to get access to content that can be tailored to their needs. ConstantContact and Silverpop, two firms that offer marketing technology and services, have APIs that allow marketing services firms to use their technology to offer advanced services to their customers. The APIs are private in the sense that they are offered as part of a business partner relationship.

This use of private APIs can morph into a public API as the creation of the business relationship becomes more automated.

Creating Internal Apps

Our experience with early adopters of APIs shows that great value can be realized when companies use APIs to create apps for internal use.

Teams create APIs to make content and services available to the rest of the company on a self-service basis. In a way, this model fulfills the vision of service-oriented architecture (SOA) that has been pursued for about 10 years. The emphasis on creating an API as a product that is intended for self-service use helps overcome some of the adoption barriers that SOA programs encountered.

When IT organizations started on the SOA journey, they didn't have many successful archetypes to guide them. Today, however, they can borrow ideas and models from thousands of public APIs powering hundreds of thousands of apps.

Private use of APIs to create apps for internal consumption can solve a huge number of problems.

Private APIs can fuel creativity internally as well. At The *New York Times*, professionals on staff use the APIs in innovative ways, according to Derek Willis. "Our interactive graphics desk can build really creative stuff with the new APIs. Some of the creative campaign profile or finance graphics would have been impossible or just a ton of manual work without the APIs. The reporters can do lookups that they couldn't have done before. This means they can ask more questions, do new kinds of analysis, and create comparisons. The API enables them to get answers where it might not have been possible before or have been too much work. This allows them to produce their core business product better—which is journalism."

Benefits of Private APIs

If you read about APIs, most often the stories you see are about how Amazon has used its APIs to create a massive channel or how Twitter has an API that has created hundreds of thousands of apps, or how Facebook's APIs have launched new kinds of industries. What you don't see is how private APIs can make it easier and faster to build apps inside your company.

In fact, we believe that private APIs provide more value than public APIs by an order of magnitude. For most businesses, private APIs will typically result in substantially more business impact than a public API. In most cases, outside of the Twitters or Googles, a public API will incrementally improve your company's business performance metrics, but a private API can transcend the public API in nearly every case. If you remember our image of the iceberg, private APIs are the large mass below the surface.

Examples of how private APIs might be used include:

- Private APIs can enable rapid and scalable development for mobile strategies, allowing each mobile product team to build apps quickly without worrying about how to populate them with content.

- There is often a pent-up demand for access to the business assets that are exposed in an API that leads to a quick return on any investment. Private APIs can help simplify an IT infrastructure to meet that demand.

- Private APIs can improve business development as they make it much easier and faster for partners to integrate (with the added benefit of making your service more sticky), requiring relatively little oversight and time from your own internal resources.

In essence, while public APIs have raised awareness about the value of APIs, the use of private APIs can improve the way that technology serves business and create tremendous value for the companies who understand how to use them.

Risks Related to Private APIs

It's not a new idea to create apps with reusable business assets and for those apps to support the business. The reason that APIs are now succeeding both in the private and public realm is that the way to make them useful has finally been discovered.

In part, APIs are now successful because they are productized, and they allow for true self-service that makes communication more efficient between the API provider and the developers who use it. The power of an API diminishes dramatically if the only people who can use it are the experts who created it. For an API to be truly useful, it must be productized so that others can use it themselves. Using an API internally does not change this principle, although some implementation details may be different.

A prominent danger in private use of APIs is not only skimping on self-service, but also failing to provide operational support that allows the API to be relied on as a production asset. You must be serious about making sure that an API is always on if you are going to provide it. If people cannot rely on the stability and speed of an API, if they cannot tell when it is working, if they are not informed of changes, developers will not rely on the API and it will fail.

Another issue related to the private use of APIs is not marketing or evangelizing it. It's just as important to actively drive adoption and evangelize private APIs to employees and partners just as you would public APIs. The point is not to just put the API out there and expect colleagues to find it and use it. It's also important to do some education about how to use the API and not assume that everyone will see and understand its applications. Regarding his work on the *New York Times* API, Derek Gottfrid said, "We did a lot of internal education. In the beginning, some organizations didn't know what an API was—one thought it stood for Associated Press International!" Brad Stenger, Developer Advocate at the *New York Times*, says that internal education is ongoing.

"If we mention APIs at any large meeting or workshop, we still provide a very basic explanation of what they are and how we use them. Although we've used APIs for years, to many they're still more unknown than well-known."

Creating a Public API Value Chain

Public APIs have gotten the most attention, and rightfully so. Even though we believe that the most effective way to leverage an API is through internal consumption, the biggest and most powerful technology companies are able to scale public APIs in amazing ways. These rare public APIs have been used to create a whole new ecosystem, the public app marketplace. Examples include the Apple App Store, the Google Android Market, social media apps like Facebook, Twitter, and Flickr, and markets for business apps like Salesforce.com's AppExchange or Google Apps Marketplace. Some of these API economies run on cash, and some have other motivations. The millions of apps that have been created are the most profound testament to the power that APIs can have to spark innovation given the right business conditions.

Public APIs have also created new ways to deliver business services. Amazon Web Services, the Rackspace Cloud, and many other providers offer cloud-computing services via APIs. Most of Salesforce.com's traffic related to its CRM app comes through APIs. The same is true for eBay.

Public APIs also can be used to support crowdsourcing, innovation, and the extension of a brand or product into a variety of niches.

Here are the basic elements of a public API value chain:

The business assets
> The owner of the business assets is usually seeking a wider audience for those assets. Public APIs are frequently used to extend a successful product into new arenas and niches that cannot be reached efficiently in other ways.

The API provider
> As stated earlier, the API provider is often the same as the owner of the business assets, but this is not always the case. In addition to designing and creating the API, the provider must create an environment in which the API can be understood and used. The provider must create some sort of incentive to encourage developers to use the API. The provider then must promote the API to developers and also promote use of the apps the developers create. The large-scale app marketplaces serve both of these purposes.

Developers
> Motivations are wide and varied for using an API. Some developers are motivated to experiment with interesting technology. Some developers are interested in public service or activism. Others are motivated by the challenge of innovating. Of course, there is always the prospect for developers to make money from a successful app.

Applications

The apps created using a public API must have a distribution channel to find an audience. Public APIs have been used to create millions of apps for diverse audiences with different needs.

Ways to Use a Public API

While it is very difficult to categorize all the ways that public APIs are providing value to the API provider, the following patterns are quite common:

- Enhancing value and extending the brand
- Reaching niche markets
- Expanding reach across platforms and devices
- Fostering innovation

Enhancing Value and Extending Your Brand

APIs can capitalize on the enthusiasm for a business asset. Twitter, for example, captured the attention of the world with its simple ability to keep millions of people in touch with each other's thoughts. Twitter's API allowed thousands of developers to put Twitter's platform to work through all sorts of apps. Some of these, like TweetDeck, became businesses in their own right. (Twitter eventually acquired TweetDeck.)

Facebook's APIs have also extended its brand and become a platform for the creation of social gaming and dozens of other types of apps. BranchOut is a competitor to Link-edIn that is based on Facebook. Zynga is well known for its popular Facebook games. The same pattern broadly applies to examples such as Google Apps, Flickr, Sales-force.com, and Box.net.

The result of making these platforms available through a public API has been an explosion of innovation. The companies with successful public APIs have been able to reach new audiences and niches, benefiting from the creative energy of thousands of developers.

Unfortunately, the success of public APIs has obscured the roles that APIs can play. Most of the successes just mentioned are based on a wave of excitement about the business asset. Creating the API helped harness that excitement in new ways. One common mistake is that companies confuse the excitement about business assets with excitement about an API. In none of the cases just mentioned did the excitement about the API precede excitement about the business asset. In other words, it does not make sense to expect an API to automatically generate interest in your business assets.

Reaching Niche Markets

Public APIs have been used to create apps to reach niche markets. eBay and Amazon have pioneered this use of APIs. Both companies published APIs to allow partners to embed product offerings in their apps and sites. Partners receive a portion of the revenue generated. This model allows a partner with access to a niche market to affordably offer the ability to buy more goods and services.

In addition, the public APIs make it easy to embed the ability to buy a product or service. A fan site could have listings of product offerings, books, and memorabilia.

This model does not have to be commercial. Any organization with interesting business assets can expose them via an API.

Expanding Reach Across Platforms and Devices

Making APIs available also allows developers with a wide variety of motivations to solve their own problems. Would a Turkish language version of your content or service be helpful but not worth the investment? By publishing and promoting an API, developers can create a program that meets specialized needs. For example, a developer created a Linux audio player for NPR on-demand. NPR likely never would have invested in this audience, but was happy to allow someone else to fill the need.

APIs make it easy to work with developers who have skills to create specialized apps. Talented developers can access the API and create apps.

One interesting aspect in expanding the reach of a business asset through an API is the motivation of the developers. It is not easy to predict what sort of apps will seem exciting to developer populations. It is usually not reasonable to expect that creating an API will automatically expand reach in any specific way.

Fostering Innovation

Public APIs can support innovation both directly and indirectly. A direct approach to supporting innovation might involve exposing some business assets through APIs and then running a contest to promote creation of solutions. Innocentive is a company that was created to execute innovation using just such a model, although not only through APIs. This form of crowdsourcing, where an API is used along with incentives, is one example of the Open Innovation models that Professor Henry Chesbrough has written about in his research.

Another way that public APIs help support innovation is by providing good ideas that can then be completed or enhanced by the API provider. At NPR, after launching an API that provided access to various types of content, an independent developer created an app for the iPhone called NPR Addict. The app was a big hit and generated more than 500,000 API content requests a month.

In addition, the lone wolf developer had limited resources. The user interface, the breadth of functionality, and the way the app was marketed and supported all fell short of what NPR could do on its own. The developer demonstrated a demand for such an app, but the terms of use for NPR's content restricted any way of sharing revenue to give the independent developer incentive to build the app in a more robust way. NPR then developed its own iPhone app, extending the NPR brand in ways that NPR Addict could not.

The internal development of public apps can also work the other way around when a company develops an app to demonstrate what is possible with an API in order to inspire developers. The value proposition of internal development is that you have the power of the brand and a team of knowledgeable people who care passionately. No one's going to do the job better than you.

Benefits of Public APIs

Innovation and brand awareness are obvious potential benefits that public APIs can offer. But don't discount the value that they can provide around recruiting and public relations. Being at the forefront of technology and being open about those efforts draws people into the company and gets them excited about it. If people are excited about this work, they may be interested in working for you to help make it better. Unlike private APIs, public APIs make it possible for potential recruits to be aware of your great work.

When considering this aspect of the public API value proposition, be thoughtful about how PR can play into it. In addition to having a public API, think about writing blog posts about the progress of the API or asking the community questions about how to make it better. In essence, a public API can generate goodwill in the marketplace, so do what you can to sustain that.

Risks Related to Public APIs

There are many different kinds of risks associated with public APIs, including legal, technical, and strategic risks. Among the less obvious risks is hinging too much of your business's success on the program. It would be easy to attribute the success that the largest players enjoy to the creation of an API program. It is absolutely true that Twitter, Facebook, eBay, and Amazon would not be as widespread and successful without their APIs, but the value of business assets motivates the use of the APIs. The biggest mistake in the use of APIs is that companies think that the interest is in the API, not in the business assets that they are offering. Then, if the API does not meet the unrealistic goals for public adoption, the program is shelved. A much better strategy for most companies is to cut their teeth using APIs internally or to support partner relationships. Then, as the value of the private API is better understood, it can be promoted for use as a public API.

Some other possible pitfalls of public APIs include:

- Rights infringement
- Attacks against the API systems
- Attacks against the content

- Potential cannibalization of your core business
- Overexposing your business assets to your competitors
- Conflicts in expectations between public developers and potential partners
- Resource allocation out of line with the value proposition

We'll talk about how to respond to some of these concerns in Chapter 4.

Shifting: Private to Public, Public to Private

We have deliberately oversimplified this discussion by assuming that private and public APIs are implemented separately and are not related. While both sorts of APIs must be able to support self-service and must be reliable, there is often very little difference in practice between the way that private and public APIs are designed, created, operated, and used.

This is a good thing because we've also found that it is hard to predict how your API will play out. An API launched as a public offering may create the most value when used as a private API (in fact, this is frequently the case). An API launched in private may be used both in private and in public.

API Evolution at the New York Times

"Our API was really developer driven from the 'bottom up,'" said Derek Gottfrid of his work on the *New York Times* API. "We started by offering a search API. We had a tightly coupled, monolithic web app, and internal developers kept using this API, so we decided to make it available to external developers. There were lots of cultural benefits—we were able to move away from monolithic app development and break up teams to develop new services."

The next step was to add more APIs to support internal changes. "Based on this experience, we added a lot more APIs, in part to support internal re-orgs. This let us get developers up to speed more quickly. In this way our APIs helped us manage an internal cultural shift."

Innovation followed. "On a parallel track in 2008," said Gottfrid, "we expanded the scope of the API to enable really cool prototyping inside the company. We wanted to show off what we did and not keep all the fun to ourselves, so we started to expose these prototypes externally."

This in turn led to new business opportunities. "Once we got some of these creative new services out in public, it was almost like lead generation for our business development group. We would get email from other companies saying that they were already doing cool stuff with our APIs and wanted to strike an arrangement. In that way, our API let a partner get productive really fast without a lot of red tape (having a standard license agreement really sped up forging those partnerships)," said Gottfrid.

The story of Netflix provides another example of such a shift. Netflix started out offering a public API, but found its greatest success with its private API.

Netflix: Public API to Private API

Netflix originally launched an API in 2008. The API was designed to allow independent developers to use metadata from the site and to let "1,000 flowers bloom." At that time, Netflix was primarily focused on the subscription service for DVD rentals. As the focus of the business shifted substantially more toward streaming, the API then became a vehicle to support internal and partner developers that would facilitate video consumption on streaming devices.

The Netflix development team used the API internally to support access to Netflix streaming content through devices from a variety of manufacturers. In many cases, the Netflix team performed the development, not the device manufacturers.

The result was a dramatic increase in the use of Netflix streaming content, as shown in Figure 3-2.

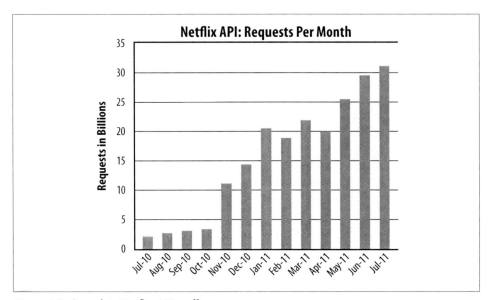

Figure 3-2. Growth in Netflix API traffic

Part of the growth in requests had to do with increased "chattiness" between the devices and the API (to support the rich and dynamic experiences for Netflix customers), but the bulk of the rise is due to the impressive rise in Netflix customers, a dramatic increase in the number of Netflix-supported devices, and the increased usage of the Netflix service per customer. In 2011, Netflix became the largest single source of traffic on the Internet in the United States (representing, by some accounts, at least 30 percent of the total Internet traffic during peak hours). Even more dramatic, traffic from the public API is just a tiny sliver of the total Netflix traffic. The preponderance of traffic comes from the private API.

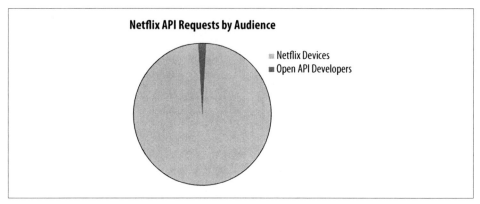

Figure 3-3. Netflix traffic by audience

API Business Models for Working with Partners

With this understanding of private and public APIs in place, the chapter now explores API business models for working with partners.

Expanding Reach: More Apps, More Platforms

Developers who create apps using your API can create new business channels. By allowing partners to build apps using your API, more apps can be created, expanding your application portfolio. For example:

- Salesforce.com has a thriving collection of applications on its AppExchange that enhance and extend the reach of its core product.
- Twitter has more than 300,000 registered applications in various states of development.

Right now there is an explosion of mobile devices such as phones and tablets, but living room devices such as DVRs, Blu-ray players, and gaming consoles as well as public kiosks and automobiles are also driving new channels for distributing content.

Whether your company is in retail, news, entertainment, games, or any other industry, there is likely an opportunity to offer an app on at least some of these platforms. Not only do these implementations extend the brand, but they also help companies reach new audiences or the same audiences in different ways.

AccuWeather's Chris Patti cites increased reach as an important benefit of working with partners. "Our partners create reach that we never could have had without an API," says Patti. "And they push us to have new products that get unveiled on a platform. We've been able to use the API to innovate together with partners. They innovate on the frontend and we can innovate on the backend with our API as the content provider. This has changed our development—we are now almost doing joint development with partners. The API is now almost a line of business itself. It's become like a product that is one of the main ways that someone experiences our brand."

Gaining Indirect Revenue

Revenue sharing is an emerging model for marketplaces with certain characteristics. Not every marketplace supports this model, but it has worked for some companies that initially took a different approach. A job search engine tried charging for its API, but had few takers. When it proposed placing sponsored jobs in its API and offered to share revenue with online publishers, the demand increased substantially.

On the other hand, some marketplaces are so hot that developers will pay to put their products in the shop window. Developers who want to place their wares in the Apple iTunes store must first pay $100 and then they receive 30 percent of the sales from their products.

Increasing Innovation through Partners

Experiments by independent innovators can light the way to interesting new directions for products and services. This model allows a company to learn from partners' experiences without having to bear all the risks.

- NPR.org discovered there was a huge appetite for a smartphone application to deliver its content when they saw the traffic that the NPR Addict app was getting. NPR then created its own iPhone app, whose traffic was many times greater than NPR Addict.
- Twitter acquired Tweetie in 2010. Twitter then made Tweetie its official iPhone app. Twitter then went on to acquire TweetDeck as well.

Increasing Application Value through Integration

APIs are in many ways the "glue" of SaaS, connecting applications developed by the provider to the population that consumes those applications as a service. Companies such as Salesforce.com fall under this model. In this model, your application becomes more valuable because you can access and repurpose the data that already exists inside it and integrate and cross reference that data with data inside other systems, such as ERP. That data is accessed via APIs. More than half of all transactions in Salesforce.com occur through APIs, to which customers cannot get access until they have purchased a license.

Strictly speaking, Salesforce.com does not charge for its APIs. It charges per user—but the value of that user "seat" goes up substantially when an enterprise license, which includes the API, is purchased.

Freemium Use

Companies monetizing their API sometimes offer developers some capabilities for free, and then charge for additional functionality. Google Maps uses this model, allowing anywhere from 10 to thousands of calls per day for free, and charging for exceeding the terms of the plan.

A free API can be a great way to extend reach and brand awareness—essentially an actionable advertisement. Understandably, the concept of indefinitely giving something away into which much time and effort has been devoted makes some executives nervous. The freemium model makes this a lot more like offering free samples.

Still, there are costs to be considered. If you offer a level of free access, you have to enforce the conditions that trigger payment. It could entail:

- Metering service and producing a bill every month
- Enforcing a special rate limit and giving the third party a service-level agreement
- Inserting extra data fields if the client is willing to pay for more licensed content

You might also face additional requests:

- Support for compliance with regulations: SOX (Sarbanes-Oxley Act) compliant logging or support of HIPAA for healthcare information, or PCI (credit card compliance) for transactional APIs
- Reporting on the cost of the data served by the API

There are pros and cons to such models. You don't want to start out offering something for free and later have to back down from that position for a variety of reasons. Twitter, for example, had to do this recently. Freemium models are trickier than they look and have specialized design considerations.

Programmable Web's View of API Business Models

API business models have evolved from a few simple patterns to a much larger collection. John Musser, Editor and Founder of the ProgrammableWeb.com, has analyzed how business models for public APIs have evolved. In 2005, most API business models fell into the categories shown in Figure 3-4.

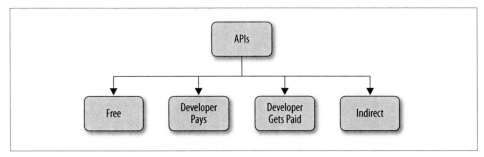

Figure 3-4. API business models circa 2005

The categories are pretty straightforward. *Free* means developers do not have to pay to use the API and that the API provider does not consider that the API has a significant business benefit. For the developer, value from the usage of free APIs can accrue from the use of the business assets, awareness of content provided, through the ability to reach new customers, or any number of other ways. For the provider, a "free" API with no significant business benefit might still add some cachet or "cool factor" to the company and the team. Of course, there are lots of good reasons to offer an API to developers for free, but these are better described under the Indirect category below. In reality, there are very few totally "free" APIs—most successful APIs are attached to some sort of business benefit, as described below.

Developer Pays means there is a charge for using the API. In this model, the developer uses the API to create something they or their organization wants. For the Developer Pays model to work, the business assets exposed must have high value and the API provider must allow that value to be leveraged by developers. The benefit to the API provider is compensation directly from the developer (as well as through reaching new people who use the developer's apps).

Developer Gets Paid means that developers receive some sort of revenue share or direct payment as an incentive to use the API. In this model, the applications created must generate some value, either by creating new revenue from end-users or some other sort of quantifiable benefit that the API provider and the developer share. The business assets exposed must have value too, either directly or indirectly, so that the API provider can share some of the revenue with the developers.

Indirect means that the use of the API achieves some goal that drives the core business model, provides value such as increasing awareness of specific content, or drives sales of existing products. For example, a retailer may offer "product catalog" and "store locator" APIs with the idea that they will increase store visits and online sales. Or, distributing news content more widely through apps will increase clicks back to the destination website, increasing advertising revenue.

The provider of the business assets and the developers may be on a mission to promote some content or activity, or some other motivation may be in play. In reality, most APIs that are "free" for developers to use create value indirectly, which is why this category exists. (After all, not many companies today can afford to engage in activity that has no business benefit!)

From these basic categories, many different types of business models emerged as shown in Figure 3-5.

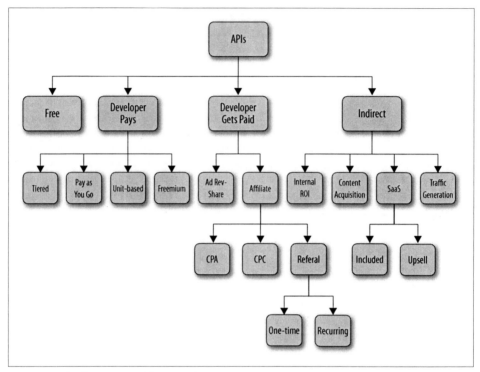

Figure 3-5. API business models circa 2011

While the *Free* model is still the same, the other three types of business models evolved into more specialized categories.

The *Developer Pays* model has variants that require developers to pay for different levels of usage (*Tiered*), to pay a fee based on usage (*Pay as You Go*), to pay according to the consumption of specific units of computing or service (*Unit*), or to use the API for free but pay for various types of additional services (*Freemium*).

The *Developer Gets Paid* model has been the focus of quite a bit of evolution that falls into two categories: *Ad Revenue Share*, which is a straightforward split of advertising revenues generated by an application, and *Affiliate*, which has several variants. The most common sort of affiliate program offers a reward for some specific activity. *Cost Per Action (CPA)* provides a fee for some sort of action desired by the provider of the API, such as a purchase, a subscription, providing an email address, and so on. *Cost*

Per Click (CPC) rewards the affiliate for traffic that goes to specific pages. The *Referral* model can provide a *One-time* reward or a share of *Recurring* revenue.

The *Indirect* model has evolved and although rather hidden in Figure 3-5, the most important category of all is internal ROI, value that is internal to an organization (see sidebar). *Internal ROI* happens when an API serves a useful purpose inside an organization.

The Value of Internal ROI

The business model that is most underreported but which harbors the most potential impact is the internal ROI model, a subset of the indirect model shown in Figure 3-5. If we have any qualms about Musser's diagram, it's that this business model appears as just one of many. While this may be true in terms of actual numbers of business model types, the Internal ROI model represents the vast majority of the underwater mass in the iceberg analogy.

Many leading enterprise are reinventing their internal infrastructure to be more like a Facebook, a Google, an Amazon, or a Twitter. They're using lightweight APIs as a way to let employees more quickly build applications for private or partner use. They are also using the same APIs to drive their core businesses.

Jason Sirota, Director of Application Architecture at XO Group Inc., formerly known as The Knot Inc., says that their API is mostly designed to benefit internal development. "Specifically, the API has two objectives—to reduce internal coupling across three to four lines of business and create well defined interface points that are RESTful, as opposed to tightly coupled based on .NET. We took this direction because we're moving to a world of heterogeneous clients." The internal ROI angle is the main focus at present but that could change. "While today we only expose the APIs to internal and mobile developers, eventually we think there are wins in taking this API outside the ecosystem," says Sirota.

AccuWeather uses its API for partner development, but also for internal development. According to Chris Patti, director of technology at AccuWeather, "An API lets us compartmentalize development. We focus on giving them the best data and developers can focus on the killer UI. The developer has the power and control in their own hands. The API has really changed our ability to respond to our own user base."

Leading enterprises recognize that in traditional IT, computing resources are scarce and cycle times are treated as scarce (which is why initiatives take months or even years). In a leading web company like a Google or Facebook, they've realized that computing resources are essentially ubiquitous, and so their internal infrastructure, designed largely around APIs, allows cycle times of weeks or even days to quickly create apps for new initiatives.

Content Acquisition refers to an API providing valuable information to the API provider, either data entered through an application or monitoring of some activity worth observing. For *SaaS* applications, an API can be *Included* as an extra benefit or be part of an *Upsell* to a higher level of service. Finally, an API can be part of a program of *Traffic Generation* for a website or even for a physical store.

CHAPTER 4

Crafting Your API Product Strategy

APIs should not be geeky "science projects." They are critical business tools. Successful APIs need clear objectives that relate directly to business objectives and track closely to key performance indicators (KPIs) for the business at large.

Strategy can mean many different things. When it comes to APIs, it is reasonable to speak about business strategy, implementation strategy, technology strategy, operational strategy, and promotional strategy. This chapter focuses on business strategy and specifically on crafting your initial vision of how creating an API will actually help achieve business goals. This chapter will answer the following questions:

- What is your business objective in creating an API?
- What is the vision for your API?
- What questions should be answered to create a comprehensive API strategy?
- What types of API strategies are being pursued?
- What objections should you be prepared to handle about APIs?

Establish a Clear Business Objective

First, and fundamentally, the key question to answer relates to exactly why you have decided to create an API to begin with.

What is the business purpose of the API? What are you trying to achieve? What problem are you trying to solve? What opportunity are you trying to take advantage of?

These are the fundamental business questions your strategy must answer, and they hearken back to an even more fundamental issue: your corporate vision statement and your vision for the API.

Have a Vision for Your API

Like any other product or major project, it is critical to foster a common understanding of what you are trying to accomplish. This is why the first step to successful API programs is to create a common vision for your API.

 Create a common vision for your API.

To some, a vision statement might seem too much like management-speak, but having a clear definition of success can go a long way toward creating buy-in and focus for your team.

A vision statement can help identify the top priorities: what must be done and more importantly, what should not be done. This becomes especially crucial down the road, as you clarify progress versus expectations for the project (especially if you get off to a slow start) as well as to avoid your team being pulled in different directions by competing interests (a significant risk, especially if your program starts to take off).

If you don't have a good example of a vision statement on hand, here are some important things to consider:

- What is the ideal end-state and business objective?
- What are the important things to do day-to-day to get there?
- What are the three key metrics that measure success?
- What are the important things to do day-to-day to continue to meet the objectives over time?

If you can express these concisely—on one slide or one page—the vision statement can be a valuable tool to measure progress and focus resources.

We spoke with Steve Smith and Chris Patti about the motivation for creating Accu-Weather's API. "Not every country in the world has the same quality of public services that we do. Our user base is anyone on the planet, so a farmer in India should be able to pick up the phone and get a heads up if bad weather is headed his way. Right now that farmer might have nothing. Our vision for the API is real time, localized content to the individual, in any corner of the globe, in the right language."

Corporate vision and API vision should align, and AccuWeather's lines up perfectly. "The vision for the API is consistent with our vision for the company: 'Save life and property' To achieve this, we want to change how the content gets into the API. We want to be innovative in updating content in real time (example: thunderstorm data), and make sure we give back the freshest data with one call."

Similarly, the *New York Times* API offers a good example of a vision statement. "The API has reoriented the company in how they view a classic old industry," said Derek Gottfrid, now of Tumblr. "One thing that really helped was that we were able to tie the mission of the API to the core mission statement of the NYT: 'To collect, create, and distribute information.' In many ways the API is the purest sense of that vision and best practices," said Gottfrid. "Once we saw the API as supporting the core mission, the NYT started to think of their entire business in a new way. This was about delivering information, just not using trucks to deliver papers."

API Strategy Basics

Business assets such as information, a product, or a service, can be made accessible through an API. The next step is for someone to create a new, or modify an existing, app or site that uses the API in a way that provides value to an audience. When people use the applications supported by the API, the API provides value to the company.

The key questions to start any discussion of API strategy are therefore:

- Who will use the API? (Internal staff, partners, or external developers)
- What assets could be made available through an API?
- Who should have access to each type of available asset?
- How should the API make those assets available?
- What types of applications could be constructed using the API?
- What will motivate developers to use the API to create applications?
- How would those types of applications create value for everyone involved?
- How will the audience discover the applications?

In other words, before striking out with an API program, step back and ask: "What makes sense for the business?" In our experience, in most API programs, the initial strategy is only a starting point. There can be many surprises along the way and innovation and agility are two key benefits of having an API. Although having a strategy is important, if you have some business justification for moving forward, you might consider taking a calculated risk about the possible unknown benefits of creating an API —particularly for internal use where the ROIs we have seen are huge.

In creating a strategy, look at your markets. In general, each market where a company operates has one or more segments where the company is gaining, holding steady, or losing share. Common business objectives include:

- Accelerate share growth
- Move from stagnancy to share growth
- Reverse share losses

Of course, not all API providers are commercial businesses and not all benefits impact the bottom line. For example, NPR's goal in creating an API was to improve the services provided to internal teams, member stations, partners, and the general public in an effort to improve its public-service mission.

APIs Need a Business Sponsor

The most successful API strategies have a business sponsor. From what we've seen, API projects without a business sponsor generally have a lot more difficulty acquiring funding and ultimately starting the work.

Undoubtedly, there are developers in every organization and in the surrounding community who are inspired by the prospect of using a new and exciting API. We encourage this—but only if the innovation can be justified with a business objective. The business-to-developer (B2D) initiative is not usually generated by the business, but rather a technologist who is passionate about creating new functionality. Innovation is important, but if it can be attached to an objective that increases the likelihood of achieving KPIs from somewhere inside the business—"improve customer satisfaction" or "improve branding," for example—it has a greater chance of securing the business sponsorship needed, which again, dramatically improves the chance of success.

At Sears, an innovative API project was justified by a mandate that the top two partners for the company communicate through the API. Despite being primarily intended as an innovation platform for developers, the project was justified on a B2B basis.

Business sponsors place developers, both internal and external, under the gun, peppering them with questions such as, "How quickly can you come up with your first app?" and "When will I see ROI?" The business sponsor can help develop metrics to keep the project moving forward and help get additional resources if they are needed.

Types of API Strategies

We categorize API usage in two dimensions: by who uses the API to create applications and by who uses the applications developed using the API. In each dimension, developers and users could be private staff, partners, or members of the public at large. The most important dimension for most companies introducing an API to execute strategy is the second: Who are the customers and how will they use applications? By knowing how your customers will use applications, you can better understand what kinds of apps you should be building with your API (or encouraging others to build).

The following section sets forth considerations and questions to keep in mind if you choose to pursue private or public API strategies. It also discusses exposing your API to partners.

Use Your Own API

Using your own APIs creates efficiencies. If one API can be designed to handle all inbound and outbound interfaces with your company, supporting that API is much easier than management of support resources. If new versions need to be created for different audiences, it requires more maintenance.

For example, at NPR, the organization created one large API and a tiered rights-management system so that different users and developers would get different content even though there was only one "pipe" to maintain.

Moreover, experimenting privately with your APIs establishes trust with other people using it because they understand that if you are committing your most important assets to it, your partners and outside developers can feel confident that the "rug" will not be pulled out from under them.

Private API Strategies

When an organization sets a strategy for a private API, the objective may be to foster innovation or to save money and improve efficiency. It is not uncommon for the improvements from a private API to find their way into a public API. That is why we encourage API successes to be publicized within the organization; they may have implications for external use.

One of the main goals of private APIs is to end bottlenecks, where groups with special expertise tightly control assets. By opening up access to assets to any (and potentially every) group within the organization, the assets can be used to their fullest potential. Currently, the most influential example of this kind of leverage power is in exposing valuable assets through an API to mobile development teams. Once the API is established and in full swing, all mobile teams can work on their own cycles to build the products that they need, without waiting as much on changes from dependent services like an internal database application. Again, because private APIs can also be exposed to partners as well, the limitation here will be with app development resources not with the constraints of the API.

Another emerging example where organizations can take advantage of APIs is by allowing internal developers to create innovative dashboard apps for use by project managers and executives. Groups that do not have technology staff can hire consultants to create applications to meet their needs. With an API in place, in addition, applications that make good use of APIs can be propagated across the organization.

Public API Strategies

Public API strategies have had a huge impact on a small set of very influential businesses that can attract sufficient developer attention, such as Google, Amazon, and Twitter. A public API creates an opportunity with unpredictable rewards. Here, the primary objective centers on the scale of adoption.

Public API providers ask themselves the following questions around their primary motivations, which also become success factors for the APIs:

- Does the public API play a key role in your overall business strategy (as it did with Twitter) or is it an ancillary business?
- What level of staffing and engagement are you willing to fund to support the public developer community?
- How does the public API get prioritized against other products?
- If you also run a private API, how do they relate to each other, both technically and in terms of business priority?
- What skills are already in house for a public API and what skills need to be obtained?

The practical questions to achieve these factors include:

- How do we scale the developer support staff?
- How can we enable the community to take care of itself and give them credit for doing so?

For all the major players we know of, internal use of the API outstrips public use by a substantial margin. In other words, if your public API is successful, your infrastructure is likely going to experience traffic from both types of applications.

Putting Together a Team

Once you establish your vision, mission statement, and strategy around the API program, you are ready to assemble a team to execute on the strategy.

A successful API program is driven by like-minded people who understand the potential that the API offers the business. The team should include a few specific roles (see Table 4-1) as well as a group of committed developers and operations personnel. With a strong team in place, the resulting API will be much more robust and the seeds of a vibrant community more easily planted.

Of course, at the beginning of an API program, each team member may have multiple roles until the team is able to grow. Some roles (like legal) are more consultative than part of the team in most cases.

Table 4-1. Roles in an API Team

Role	Tasks	Qualifications
Developer Evangelist	Sells the idea to all stakeholders: internal and external	Must be technically savvy enough to understand the API and what it can do
	Gets out from behind desk to engage with developers	Passionate about building cool apps with the API
	Gets the support of an executive sponsor	Strong marketing instincts and good judgment in representing your brand
		Effective social skills both online and offline
Product Manager	Creates overall product roadmap	Ability to rapidly prioritize competing requirements
	Facilitates decisions about features	
	Understands how API is performing for customers and business	Ability to understand and simplify customer requirements
	Drives API improvements	
Community Manager	Often the same person as the developer evangelist	
Engineers	Design the API	Experience in API design
	Write the API	Knowledge of JSON, XML
	Provide technical support for the API	
Quality Assurance	Validates that the API is delivering the output as expected	Understanding of dependencies and how to interact with customers
		Experience in test development and continuous integration
Marketing and legal	Provides branding guidelines for using the API	Understanding of developers and the company's marketing strategy
	Promotes the API	
		Ideally, understands developer communities
Legal	Provides rules and guidelines for using the API	Understands developers and technology
	Defines appropriate use of corporate data and customer data	
	Vets any content licensed from third-parties	

The Developer Evangelist

Behind almost every great API program is a great developer evangelist. A developer evangelist makes it their personal mission to make developers using the API successful and to provide the API team with feedback to make the API better. The best developer evangelists are extroverted, technical people who get out in the developer community and frequent the same online and offline forums as key influential developers and thought leaders. This applies equally to a company with a private API—you must convince internal developers to adopt your API, and you need their feedback.

What do you look for in a developer evangelist?

- First and foremost, a great passion for building cool apps with your company's API
- Strong marketing instincts and good judgment in representing your brand
- Technical skills (coding experience is a plus) that can relate to developers and their feedback and represent this to your API team accurately
- Social skills that can be effective in both online social forums and offline developer events, such as hackathons

You are looking for someone who can find developers and connect them with each other. This gives a small team the power to make a large group of developers successful with your API.

API programs that lack a developer evangelist typically have a hard time getting off the ground. Many companies mistakenly assign a nontechnical marketing manager who tries to cover the responsibilities part-time. This is not a good formula for winning the respect of programmers. If an evangelist cannot demand the respect of internal developers, how can they engage the external developer community?

Where can you find great developer evangelists? Often they are right under your nose, inside your company. You might first look for an internal developer who has a passion for building apps with your company's data and APIs. You can also reach out to and get to know some of the great developer community managers for other API programs; not only will you get a feel for what kind of person you are looking for, but they may make a connection that can help you find your ideal evangelist.

We asked Kin Lane, API evangelist for Mimeo.com, who also runs apievangelist.com, about his view of this role. "Having an open public presence for developers is really important," says Lane. "I blog and tweet in real time, as I'm building and coding and solving problems from developers. But it's also critical to be listening and participating in key developer forums. For me this includes sites like Github and Stackoverflow. In the general open world this includes Twitter, Facebook, my blog and guest writing for other blogs. Doing this in real time is critical. You can't go silent for 2 weeks while you're at an event or you'll lose credibility."

Kin emphasizes the importance of evangelism for working with partners. "With partners, I need to always be educating them. Not only on my API, but also bringing to the table other complementary APIs and what is happening in the API space," says Lane. "I also make sure I'm pointing them to any private resources they need. Many of your partner's developers may be mandated to work with your API. You need to focus on their vested interest in making it work."

In terms of internal accountability, Lane says evangelism cuts across all departments. "I have to report to all departments—technical, business, sales and marketing—to make sure they understand the opportunity and impact of the API and decisions related to it. Again, this also includes educating them on the existence of other APIs, for example, APIs that drive mobile development, so that they don't reinvent the wheel. I constantly reassess the API program all the time. The investment and return of the API program is constantly evaluated, so I need to be constantly reassessing and selling the API program internally."

Often the developer evangelist and the community manager are the same person. If not the same person, they should be very close in technical expertise, personality style, and willingness to go the extra mile to help developers use the API effectively.

Objections to APIs

An API strategy that involves offering some applications to the public may raise some eyebrows. After all, what if the API just cannibalizes existing channels and redistributes existing traffic?

Table 4-2 summarizes common objections we've heard and provides responses.

Table 4-2. Objections to APIs

Objection	Response
We are afraid our content may be misused	Content available via a well-managed API is at less risk than content on a website. You can identify a particular abusive user and shut them down, or if an inappropriate app is written, you can deny API access to the whole app.
We are afraid of the load on our systems	Load on systems is a good problem to have. It usually means that your audience is growing, either in unique users or in loyalty metrics. If not, then it means that your systems need substantial tuning. In any case, there is something very valuable to be gained here. Moreover, utilizing techniques like rate limiting can offset any concerns around server load. Using third-party vendors to help manage the infrastructural part of the API is also an option.
We are afraid of security threats	Security threats exist with any system exposed outside of a company's firewall. Whatever measures are taken to safeguard against such threats on the website should be taken against the API as well.
We are afraid page views (and ad revenue) will go down	This should be part of your cost/benefit analysis. How much money do you expect to lose? How can you protect yourself against that? From our experience, you are more likely to grow your audience through the API program than to lose revenue opportunities. The bigger your audience, the more ad impressions you are likely to serve.
We are afraid of how our brand will be used	An important facet of creating an API is making sure your brand is represented properly. This can be handled in the terms of use of the API, requiring proper attribution with your content. You can also embed such attribution in key fields as they get distributed. Generally, developers are more than happy to adhere to any such rules.

Objection	Response
We are afraid that we will be overexposing our business assets to our competitors	Understanding your competitive advantages and protecting them is a critical aspect of your API design and offering. Using rights management can enable you to expose the right assets to the right audiences, allowing you to protect yourself from your competitors.
We are afraid that we will create conflicts in expectations between the public developers and potential partners	If you maintain key partner relationships through your API program, it is possible that a public API could compromise your negotiating power with them. The partners may have everything they need in the public API, so why would they pay you for access to it? Understanding the boundaries of each audience and establishing clear terms about how they can operate is critical to serving these audiences effectively.
We are afraid that support costs for different API audiences will be higher than expected and may not be cost-effective	If you are exposing different APIs to different audiences, it is likely that one of these audiences has a higher priority than another. If you are leveraging a private API for your mobile strategy, it is likely that the internal development teams account for a much larger percentage of the overall traffic than the public developers. Meanwhile, your API team has limited time and resources to address the needs of the various audiences. It is important to consider audience prioritization when determining which tasks to focus on. It is also important to communicate effectively what the various audiences should expect in terms of responsiveness to requests.

NPR Overcomes Objections to a Public API

Initially NPR was concerned that opening a public API would enable outside parties to draw content from non-NPR products, which could end up sabotaging NPR's page views. This had implications for revenue since each page view could generate ad impressions. If an end user consumes an NPR story on a page hosted by someone else, NPR would lose the opportunity to convert the page view into an ad impression. Ultimately, NPR decided that the risk of limiting the reach of NPR content was more serious than any potential cannibalization of page views. NPR's differentiating product is audio. If someone sees a full-text link to NPR and clicks through to the audio—which embeds an ad within the first 30 seconds—the NPR API succeeded and at least the audio ad impressions are preserved.

Meanwhile, NPR's total page view traffic grew by 100 percent (see Figure 4-1) after the API took off from internal use. Leveraging the API internally enables tremendous growth potential, even while offering a public API.

NPR was able to add 80 percent more total page views in this timeframe while continuing to grow traffic on NPR.org. That suggests that mobile traffic was not cannibalizing the traffic of the main site. Rather, these page views were additive. And for a company like NPR, which generates revenue on banner ads for their news articles, this type of page view growth has a direct correlation to the bottom line.

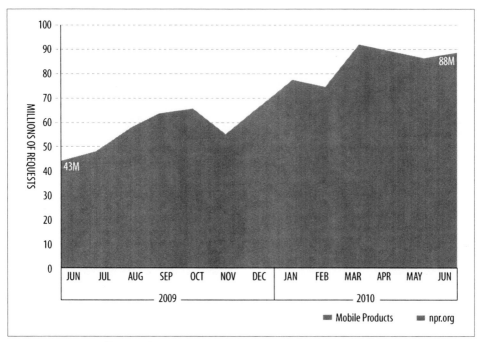

Figure 4-1. NPR traffic growth in requests per month

The *New York Times* faced some similar objections when deciding to open parts of its API for public use. "After much internal debate, we released some parts of the API externally," said Derek Willis. "There needed to be some persuasion that this wasn't a bad thing. We wanted to make sure we weren't just giving content away."

"Once we started doing public data APIs, we had a long discussion around the terms of service and how they might differ across different types of data. We also had to think through not only the benefits but also the different demands and use cases of different types of partners and developers. For example, we didn't offer the full text of articles in the public APIs for quite a while; the first API was an article search that returned just a short truncated article. Even now, most of our public API usage is for large partners, such as Amazon," said Willis.

CHAPTER 5

Key Design Principles for APIs

API design is an art in the early stages of its evolution. Nevertheless, enough experience has been amassed to develop a meaningful list of mistakes to avoid as well as some principles of success. In order to properly design your API, you're going to need to consider most of the topics in this book. Your strategy influences the design. Your audience influences the design. The very business assets you plan to expose influence the design. And of course, the technological approach that you take influences the design. This chapter focuses on three areas:

- Designing an API for different audiences
- Providing an overview of technology considerations
- Highlighting high-level design considerations

API strategy mainly focuses on creating one or more channels with your API in order to help you achieve your business goals. When people use an API, they're not really thinking about the value of the API itself. They're interested in the value of what they get through the API: the business assets (products and services) accessed through that API. In designing APIs, we attempt to provide business assets to developers so that they can create applications that deliver value to end users, who will then be able to provide some kind of value to complete the cycle of the API economy.

In general, the top APIs are carefully designed, easy to learn, logically structured, and internally consistent so that developers can guess how to bridge gaps in their understanding with relative success. An API should be a bit like a car. Every car has a steering wheel, brake pedals, and an accelerator. You might find that hazard lights, the trunk release, or radio are slightly different, but it's rare that an experienced driver can't figure out how to drive a rental car.

Designing APIs for Specific Audiences

As with any business campaign, an API needs a defined audience. In fact, there are two basic audiences for APIs to consider.

Developers (or even more broadly product and technical teams) are the *direct audience* that consumes the API and builds applications against it.

The end users are the *indirect audience* that uses the applications created using the API.

To define the audience, you should start by reflecting on your API vision statement to determine what the API is trying to accomplish. From there, you can determine which of these audience types will benefit from the API and what that interaction model needs to look like. Is it being designed for departments that rely on information from your ERP system? Mobile developers? Your top 10 partners? Affiliate marketers?

Perform an end user and/or developer segmentation analysis and force-rank priority segments. If the initial answer is "everybody," we suggest thinking a little more carefully, at least in terms of prioritization.

The challenge is to design for both developers who will create the API and end users who will use the API. Here we take a moment to explore the concerns of both.

Designing for Developers

Developers come in many stripes and subcategories. An API can be targeted narrowly toward a very specific, highly trained developer population that uses a specific technology, or to anyone in the world to whom the company would like to provide access to its business assets. Therefore, it makes sense to understand the segmentation of the developer category. Once that segmentation is understood, the choice of technical platform will become clearer.

In other words, teams who build APIs will generally have to make many technical choices—SOAP or REST? XML or JSON? OAuth or something else? The answers, more than anything else, will depend on the technical audience consuming the API. We do have some recommendations though.

Our Technology Recommendations for APIs

Unless there are specific reasons otherwise, the first choices for any API team today should be, essentially:

- "Pragmatic REST," for the structure, because it makes an API easier to learn, consume, and expand than other technologies like SOAP (we will discuss REST and "pragmatic" REST variations later)
- JSON, for the format of the data that the API consumes and returns, because it is easier to produce and consume by programmers
- OAuth, for security, because it prevents password propagation around the Internet, while supporting a variety of ways to authenticate the end user

---

If these technologies aren't familiar to you now, don't worry—we will address REST and JSON later in this chapter and OAuth (and other security topics) in Chapter 6.

Furthermore, we describe these technologies as a first choice, not as an only choice. Modern application servers and API platforms make it possible to support more than one, such as providing an API that supports both XML and JSON or that exposes both SOAP and REST APIs.

Technical Best Practices from the Tumblr API

Are there any technical best practices from the Tumblr API you'd like to share?

We want our API to be easy to learn without documentation—the way we lay out our URIs, you should just be able to drop into a command live.

We try to only slightly tweak the API. One of the big ironies of a website is that I can change it whenever I want, but an API is very brittle in that you can break your developers' applications. Versioning is an ongoing task.

Derek Gottfrid, Director of Product, Tumblr

Although REST, JSON, and OAuth are the right place to start when considering an API, there are reasons to go against these defaults.

REST might result in "chattier" or more rigid interactions between the clients and the API. There may be better ways to achieve a similar result but with greater efficiency.

JSON's slimmer object model is preferred in many cases to reduce byte count, which improves performance in delivering the bytes across HTTP. That said, XML offers the potential for richer markup and semantic options. Moreover, there are many more standards in organizing content for XML than JSON, which means that parsing applications and other code libraries could improve efficiency in developing apps.

OAuth is excellent for securing API transactions, but it is best suited for large groups of unknown developers trying to access your API. If your target audience is a small group of internal developers, OAuth may be overkill.

The key in making these decisions lies in understanding who is going to use the API and how they are going to create applications of interest to end users.

Designing for Application Users

The more you can understand what type of access end users want, the more information you will have about what to include in the API and how to make that access as easy as possible. API publishers should be thinking about what users want from their business assets and how the publisher can provide access to jumpstart the API economy.

It's difficult to generalize because it's often not clear what kinds of applications will be built, and you may have only a vague idea of the end users' latent desire for the business assets. Moreover, once APIs get launched, if they are successful, they tend to inspire new ideas and uses that may not have been considered prior to launch. This is the case for private and public APIs.

For example, popular functions, such as retrieving all the tweets from a single person (Twitter API) or creating a map with a location pinned on it (Google Maps API) can be consumed very easily because many applications perform these simple tasks. Other, more complicated functions were added later or discovered to be useful through continued expansion of the user base. The bottom line is: The more you know about the end user population and the kind of applications they want, the more informed you'll be when making choices about what functions to offer first.

NPR Knows Its Audiences

NPR set out on its API program with a good sense of its target audiences. Essentially, four groups benefit from NPR's foresight:

- *NPR staff* is the largest consumer of the API, which supports the entire infrastructure of NPR.org, the main website as well as other digital properties. The API was initially used to improve the website's backend content management system (CMS) to allow for custom feeds developed by the Editorial and Design departments. The biggest use of the API has been to build a wide range of NPR-branded applications for mobile and other platforms, resulting in 100 percent page view growth across all digital properties in less than one year.

- *NPR member stations* constitute an important share of the audience, using the API to receive content and create mashups of local and national content for their communities.

- The NPR API created new opportunities for *partners* because the API had low integration costs. This meant that existing opportunities were also easier to maintain and grow because the channel of communication was more robust than in the past when they were often handled through custom XML feeds, RSS, or other less-than-optimal methods.

- The *general public* is the fourth beneficiary of NPR's API. Extending the API helped support NPR's public service mission and provided a set of widgets and tools that has supported the creation of third-party websites that repurpose NPR content in innovative ways.

Best Practices for API Design

In our experience, some things work and some things don't when it comes to APIs. This section offers a few of what we consider solid best practices for API design.

Differentiate Your API

First things first—why should a developer use your API? How is it different from other alternatives? Why should they use it?

Here are some possible ways to differentiate your API:

- The data is unique, more complete, or more accurate than that of your competitors
- You offer better support or an easier signup process
- Your API is more robust, reliable, cooler, or faster than alternatives
- Your terms are more developer friendly; perhaps you offer more data traffic for free or at better rates

Emphasize why someone should use your API, rather than an alternative. An alternative could be a competitor's API for a public API, or an alternative data source or older (and more familiar) technique for a private API. You can also differentiate offerings and incentives around your API. One strategy is to offer different tiers of pricing based on amount or type of usage. This strategy allows you to reach more levels of subscribers. Some API calls can be free, while others may require payment. You could authorize free use of the API in a public-facing app while charging for using it behind a firewall.

Make Your API Easy to Try and Use

If your API is one of many options, your audiences may dedicate only a few minutes to trying it. If they can't make almost immediate progress, they'll go elsewhere. Successful API programs remove all barriers to use. There are a few ways to do this.

For private APIs, it is important to demonstrate real value in running a system or app off of the API. For example, the API could offer much more flexible access to content, better overall performance, more nimble development cycles, or some other benefit. To get some momentum on its adoption, identify a discrete use case for a significant app and work on getting that case operational in a production environment. Once in production, you will be able to tune it and show its value. Once a demonstrable case is live, it is easier to point to it as an example for others to follow. Moreover, the developers who implemented that first case will help evangelize for you, provided the experience was a good one. And don't forget to get buy-in from the appropriate executive and/or management teams to help grease the wheels.

For public APIs, one approach is to offer some level of free access. Many developers won't even consider using your API if there are only paid options. At this point in the customer acquisition cycle, the developer may not know if your API meets their needs or if their app's business model will support paid access.

Successful programs also make it extremely easy and fast to try the API, offering immediate gratification whenever possible. Developers visiting Twitter's API are presented with a console that enables immediate testing. Twitter takes this a step further by offering some API operations that don't require any signup or authentication (such as the public timeline operation which lets developers access the most recent status updates from all public users around the world).

If you require registration or signup for API usage, streamline the process. It's a good idea not to ask more than a few qualifying questions or implement an approval process where you must "get back to" the developer. By then, you may have already lost her attention.

This is different for private APIs, where you need a formal partner arrangement. Still, the more information you can provide to encourage partners to sign up, the better.

Make Your API Easy to Understand

The most successful APIs are designed intuitively. Simplicity is key, an axiom that applies to not only what the API can do but also to how the functions are presented to the developer. One great example is the Facebook Graph API. That API "reads like a book"; you need very little documentation to understand what you can do with the API.

An old design saying that applies well to APIs is "Make your API as simple as you can, but no simpler." Publishers often include too many functions or functions that aren't really relevant. For example, we have seen public APIs with functions that are only for internal use, such as internal code tables.

Kin Lane, developer evangelist at Mimeo, says less is more for API design. "My advice —the simpler, the better. REST, JSON, simple and straightforward services. Don't try to make it too complex. Focus on the core building blocks for an API. Do one thing, do it really well, and bundle it with simple documentation and code samples. These are the essentials of an API."

Besides offering the smallest yet richest possible set of operations, it's also critical to structure your API in a way that is easy to understand. This is a huge advantage of APIs that follow the "Pragmatic REST" patterns described below. "Pragmatically RESTful" APIs are easy to read and understand because they present API operations as human-readable URIs that can be tested with simple tools such as a web browser.

It may seem that making an intuitive, easy-to-learn, elegant API is unimportant—after all, if your API provides the right functionality, won't developers use it anyway? That might make sense until your API has competition. Application developers are picky, opinionated, and most of all, in a hurry. An elegantly designed API that they love using will win followers and happy users in a way that a more crude effort will not.

Don't Do Anything Weird

There are other aspects of simplicity that can help make your API easier to adopt. One success factor is to stick to conventions that the developer might already know.

This is especially important in the area of security. Many APIs offer custom or complex security schemes that require developers to learn them from scratch—a significant barrier to adoption. Instead, think about using common conventions such as OAuth or other commonly understood security schemes. This may not only increase adoption but also reduce your (and their) development effort.

Less Is More

Successful APIs often start with the absolute minimum amount of functionality, and then add functions slowly over time, as feedback is collected.

First, once your API is out there, it's out there. This means that once you release a piece of functionality, and developers build applications that use it—it is very, very difficult to take that piece of functionality back. With a website, all you need to do is hide a feature. With an API, reducing functionality presents the unpleasant choice of continuing to support the function for some amount of time until a quorum of developers moves on to the next improvement or iteration of that function, or risk "breaking" your developer apps and raising the ire of the developers.

Secondly, it's quite likely that the customer base will ask you to take your API in different directions than you ever imagined. This is especially the case with private APIs where internal development teams have a closer relationship with the API provider and a stronger influence. We hear this over and over again. Whether it's your strategy, the type of developer, type of app, or the specific functionality that turns out to be valuable, the API often evolves in a different direction than anticipated. In this case, starting out with the minimum level of functionality can enable the cleanest and quickest evolution of your product.

There are probably more reasons than this, but in general it's almost always a good practice to start with fewer functions and add more as needed, following the principle that less is more.

Target a Specific Developer Segment

Before thinking about the how of launching your API, think about who you are going after and what action you want them to take.

As with all good marketing programs, an API marketing campaign can be greatly helped by zeroing in on a specific segment of developers or applications you want to enable. This will help clarify and focus your strategy, tactics, resources, and how you measure success.

When talking to companies in the midst of launching an API, we often ask "Who are your target audiences?" If they answer by saying "Everybody," we get worried. Similarly, if we ask them "What kinds of apps do you expect to see built?", we get worried if their answer is, "All kinds."

Why? It's really hard to create an API to meet the demands of every possible constituent and every possible use case. And even if you had the perfect API, you can't market effectively to all these segments.

Part of the appeal of an API, private or public, is that it enables developers to innovate in ways that the API provider may not anticipate. That said, when launching the API, it is important to have expectations about how the service will likely be used so that you can launch an API that satisfies use cases. For each use case, figure out who the target segment audiences will likely be and design for those audiences.

After you have success with your first segment, you can add new partners, which in turn will enable you to extend your design to support their particular needs. If you're launching a public API, do some research into the breakdown of your developer demographics—by language or by type of app platform.

Technical Considerations for API Design

This section describes some philosophical and technical design issues that have broad implications for the way your API will operate.

REST

Various forms of REST, or Representational State Transfer, are currently the preferred style for writing APIs. The REST style was developed as a PhD dissertation by Roy Fielding, who was one of the authors of the HTTP protocol.

In essence, Fielding proposed using HTTP for inter-computer communications. Consequently, REST is based on the HTTP standard. Using the building blocks of HTTP, it divides the namespace into a set of "resources" based on unique URI patterns and uses the standard HTTP verbs—GET, POST, PUT, and DELETE—to map operations on top of those resources. These standard HTTP verbs map to the verbs create, read, update, and delete, familiar to generations of programmers as CRUD.

URIs and URLs: What's the Difference?

In the world of web standards, a URI, or Uniform Resource Identifier, is a generic reference to a "resource" on the network. It may be a very specific reference that describes the network protocol to use to reach the reference, how to reach it on a network, and where to look for it—for instance, *http://www.oreilly.com/books/api.html* is a URI. A URI can also be much more generic—one such subset is called a URN, or Uniform Resource Name, which is just a unique ID for an object.

In the history of the Internet, the term URL (Uniform Resource Locator) was frequently used to refer to a type of a URI that includes a network protocol. Technically this usage is correct, but the Internet standards world has been gradually shifting to the use of the term "URI" to refer to such references instead. We will stick with this definition in this book and consistently use the term "URI."

In REST, the URI uniquely refers to a resource or an object, or a collection of objects. Fielding formalized this structure and made it into a simple way to design an API that would work on any machine or operating system. For example, a computer program on machine A wants to look at a list of customers. It knows that there is a resource, defined by a URI, where it can get that list. All of the actions that can be performed on the entity "customer"—such as "delete" or "add"—are accessed via links and represented as XML. (As originally proposed by Fielding, XML and hypertext are key parts of REST.)

Today, nearly every computing platform can talk to an HTTP server, and the best REST-style APIs require hardly more than basic HTTP support to operate. Contrast this with previous approaches, like SOAP, which require a complex client stack in order to communicate with the server.

Unfortunately, like any complex computing concept, the term "REST" is subject to confusion and debate. Sometimes the term is used incorrectly, and sometimes REST advocates go too far in branding less-pure usage of the term as incorrect. We would like to address some of this confusion here.

Pure REST

REST, in its purest form, follows the dictates of Fielding's dissertation, as well as more recent papers and blog posts. Central to the REST style is the concept of "Hypermedia as the Engine of Application State," abbreviated HATEOAS.

An API that follows the HATEOAS principles represents itself using a very different contract than other types of APIs. Rather than defining a list of things that a client can do in a static document, it instead requires the client to discover the functionality that the API provides while using the API. A client that uses a REST-style API first connects to the server and performs a GET on a root URI. This URI, in turn, returns a list of additional URIs that may be used for additional operations, and so on.

In other words, the client of a REST API behaves something like this:

GET *http://api.myapi.com/*
: Returns a "welcome" document that contains a list of additional URIs.

GET *http://api.myapi.com/customers*
: The client sees that one of the links on the "welcome" document describes the way to get a list of customers, so it invokes that URI. (And if that link wasn't present, the client shouldn't use it—HATEOAS precludes the idea of "hard-coding" URIs into the client.)

POST *http://api.myapi.com/customers*
: The client sees that the GET from the previous step returned another link to a URI that may be used to add a new customer, so the client invokes that.

The client continues as before
: The idea is to never "hard code" a URI but instead to discover them from using the API.

In other words, a client that follows all the REST principles behaves just like a human browsing a website, following only the links that are presented. (On the other hand, a client that ignores HATEOAS behaves like a user who bookmarks certain pages deep within a site's URI structure. At some point, those bookmarks stop working.)

Clients and servers that follow HATEOAS principles are truly scalable and extensible. The server can change the shape and functionality of the API and even take certain functionality away without breaking the client because the client was built to adapt on the fly to server-side changes.

Pragmatic REST

If you have worked with REST APIs in the past, the preceding section may be foreign to you. You have likely worked with REST APIs that don't work this way at all, and you are probably used to hard-coding URIs rather than only using links returned by the server. This sometimes happens because so-called REST APIs aren't REST at all, but simply use JSON or XML over HTTP as a way to communicate (we will describe one such API shortly).

More often, however, this happens because the APIs were deliberately designed with a different goal in mind. They follow certain REST principles, but not all of them. These APIs are themselves easy to learn and navigate and represent the majority of public APIs. We call this approach "Pragmatic REST."

Why have many APIs been designed in this "pragmatic" way? In part it is because the HATEOAS principle places such a high bar for the client-side programmer. A programmer who, inadvertently or on purpose, hard-codes a URI path into an application may be in for a rude shock in the future, and the server-side API team may simply tell the client that they failed to follow the spec.

They can also be designed this way because modern API technology, including the use of mediation servers in between the client and the servers that host the APIs allow API providers to rewrite URIs and content on the fly, making it more practical to maintain a consistent URI structure.

Although HATEOAS is a good theoretical approach to designing an API, it may not apply in practice. It is important to take into account the audiences of the API and their possible approaches to building apps against it and factor that into your design decisions. HATEOAS, in some cases, may not be the right choice.

Pragmatic RESTful Principles

A pragmatic RESTful approach uses the best parts of the RESTful concept by recognizing that programmers want to understand what they can do with your API as quickly as possible and do it without writing a lot of extraneous code.

We suggest these principles of Pragmatic REST:

URIs matter

A well-designed URI pattern makes an API easy to consume, discover, and extend, just as a carefully designed API does in a traditional programming language. Pure REST disdains this principle in favor of HATEOAS.

Parameters matter

Use a standard and easy-to-guess set of optional parameters for each API call.

Data format matters

Make it straightforward for programmers to understand what kind of data the API expects, what kind of data it will return, and how to change that.

Return codes matter

Use 404 when a path does not resolve to a real object or collection, for instance, rather than returning a generic error code that the user must interpret in a proprietary way.

Everything else should be hidden

Security, rate limiting, routing, and so on can and should be hidden in the HTTP headers.

Establish clear conventions for versioning

For example, should the URI contain a version number, or should that be a parameter? In the absence of either, which version should be delivered? Of course, this assumes that your API uses versions at all.

Specifically, these principles suggest the following rules for URIs:

- URI paths that refer to a collection of objects should consist of a plural noun, such as /customers to refer to a set of all customers
- URI paths that refer to a single object should consist of a singular noun, followed by a unique primary key. For instance, /customers/Bob to refer to the customer with the primary ID of Bob, or /accounts/123456 to refer to account number 123456.
- It's OK to start the URI with some identifying path, such as the version number or environment.
- After the identifying path, nothing else should be in the URI but collections and objects.
- A set of standard query parameters should be used for collections in order to allow the caller to control how much of the collection that they see. For instance, use "count" to determine how many objects to return from a large collection, "start" to determine where to start counting from the beginning, and "q" as a generic free-form search over a collection of objects.

We also suggest the following rules for objects:

- Singular objects should support GET for read, PUT for update, and DELETE for delete.

- Collection objects should support GET to read back the whole or part of a collection and POST to add a new object to the collection.
- Singular objects may support POST as a way to change state. For instance, you could POST a new JSON or XML document to an object to change certain fields or trigger a state change or action without replacing the whole object.

Example: Designing with Pragmatic REST

Table 5-1 shows a shopping cart API that strays from RESTful conventions—it is neither "pure" nor "pragmatic" REST.

Table 5-1. The wrong way to REST

Task	Operation	URI
Insert new item into the cart	POST	*http://api.shopping.com/InsertNewItem*
Delete item from the cart	POST	*http://api.shopping.com/DeleteItem*
List everything in the cart	GET	*http://api.shopping.com/ListCart?cartId=X*
Get an item in the cart	GET	*http://api.shopping.com/ShowItem?cartId=X&itemid=Y*
Delete the whole cart	POST	*http://api.shopping.com/DeleteCart*

This API isn't hard to use, but you do have to learn the individual operations. This can get cumbersome if there are numerous operations or if the API evolves. Imagine what would happen if, in addition to cart, there were 50 other types of objects, and a whole set of operations to go with them. The resulting API documentation would be long and require searching the documentation for each new API call. For instance, a developer might have to learn that InsertNewItem only inserts an item into the shopping cart, while InsertNewItemIntoWishlist must be used for the customer's wish list, and so on ad nauseum.

The pragmatic RESTful shopping cart in Table 5-2 is easier to learn.

Table 5-2. Pragmatic RESTful shopping cart

Task	Operation	URI
Insert new item into the cart	POST	*http://api.shopping.com/cart/cartName*
Delete item from the cart	DELETE	*http://api.shopping.com/cart/cartName/item/itemName*
List everything in the cart	GET	*http://api.shopping.com/cart/cartName*
Get an item in the cart	GET	*http://api.shopping.com/cart/cartName/item/itemName*
Replace an entire item	PUT	*http://api.shopping.com/cart/cartName/item/itemName*
Delete the whole cart	DELETE	*http://api.shopping.com/cart/cartName*

This set of URI patterns makes it easier to extend the API in straightforward ways. For example, what if we want to list all the shopping carts in the system at any one time? We would add that via an HTTP GET to *http://api.shopping.com/carts*.

Query parameters still serve an important purpose—making it possible to specify additional options. For instance, imagine a very large shopping cart where you want to paginate the results. To look at items 20-29, you might use a URI like *http://api.shopping.com/cart/cartName?start=20&count=10*.

Sometimes REST Needs a Rest

REST is a great way to define an API that's simple to learn and grow, but just using REST doesn't make an API easy to learn and use and it doesn't automatically make an API efficient. For instance, REST APIs are often designed to field requests in a very granular way, resulting in many distinct resources that handle specific types of requests. As a result, it may take many individual API requests to build a single page on a mobile device. Since every mobile API request takes a long time and runs down the battery, a "chatty" API impairs performance and affects the user experience.

However, a more efficient API can be designed without throwing away the REST concept entirely. For example, higher-level "meta-resources" can be created that combine a number of lower-level resources into one. Another technique is called a "bulk request." For instance, to retrieve ten items from the REST API at once, send a single HTTP request that contains a list of URIs, and return all the responses, one after the other, as if all ten were made individually.

XML vs. JSON

Initially, the de facto standard format for REST APIs was XML. And even today, there are many viable scenarios where XML is the right choice. As a data model, it has been used to create standard grammars that describe some of the most complex data sets on Earth, including derivatives contracts and insurance policies, and XML authors can write grammars that pull information models from different areas, combine them into one complex document without worrying that they will conflict, validate the whole thing using standard technology, and transform and edit it using powerful tools. The industries that need this amount of power really need it.

That said, most APIs pass relatively simple programming languages back and forth, and for that JSON (JavaScript Object Notation) is much simpler for the programmers on both sides.

JSON was developed by Douglas Crockford, one of the people involved in the early days of JavaScript. Crockford decided to create a data definition language that consists of a small subset of JavaScript, bridging the gap between programming language objects and the Web. Easy to parse and translate, JSON became a popular platform for APIs because it could easily interface with web and mobile apps, which are typically built in JavaScript. Additionally, JSON is far more compact than XML. Since then, JSON parsers and generators have been developed for most programming languages and now JSON support is a standard part of many frameworks. Since JSON was designed as a subset of JavaScript, JSON objects can be easily turned into objects in most programming languages without any additional parsing code from the programmer. This is different from XML, which offers a complex and powerful data model, forcing programmers to convert even small XML documents to or from an object. XML also adds complexity to parsing engines with namespaces, attributes, variations on text encodings, and the like.

Read more about REST and JSON

The original REST dissertation can be found at *http://www.ics.uci.edu/ ~fielding/pubs/dissertation/top.htm*

The JSON specification can be found at *http://json.org/*

Versioning and API Design

The decision to make an API have a version number, or to be versionless, is an important design consideration because apps that are built atop an API depend on certain functionality working in a particular way. Effectively, an API is the embodiment of a contract between a publisher and a developer. As new API versions are released, that contract should stay intact. This fact needs to be balanced against continuous requests for feature upgrades from users and your internal ability and willingness to support older feature sets in an ongoing basis. Usually, API development teams are small and have a limited capacity for supporting new versions. While developers continually want newer, fancier versions of the API, and end users want to see the apps improve, the reality is that the development team can only support a few versions at a time.

There are many different ways to approach this problem. We'd like to suggest one small, three-step solution:

- Somewhere, prominent for each client or for each API call, include version 1. (A common way to do this is to include it in the URI path.)
- Every time you change the API, do everything you can to avoid ever incrementing the version number to 2.
- Consider having the absence of a version specification in the URI or parameter to indicate to the API to use either the first or the latest version.

This approach recognizes two things. First, that you have to work hard to keep the contract of the API intact—you may change it in ways that do not break existing applications, but in order to introduce a change that would break applications, you must explicitly plan for it. Second, it recognizes that sometimes in the life of an API, you might have to admit that you made a mistake and now need to start over with version 2.

This approach also gives you the flexibility to change the versioning when you must, but if a developer doesn't actually change the version number in their code, their requests will still be served without interruption.

Alternatively, if you are designing a version strategy for the API, and you are considering something like:

- A three- or four-digit version number
- A version number that changes every time you push a new release of the API
- A version number that will ever reach two digits, in the lifetime of your API or company
- A version number based on the date you last changed the API

You are probably doing the wrong thing. These approaches may work for applications or systems that have a very small, controlled distribution, but will create a host of issues with public and private APIs.

 Remember: An API is a contract. When you publish and document an API, you are also making a promise that you will not break existing applications without ample notification.

The version number essentially says, "Please stop using the old contract and switch to the new one." But it also says, "The old contract is still valid." Every time you do this, it will require effort from those who use the API, make them unhappy, and inevitably some of them will never make the transition, meaning their applications will break when you finally turn off the old version.

On the other hand, the longer you can use automated regression testing to ensure that you never need to increment the version count, the less time you will spend discussing versioning with your customers. That said, it also means that you will need to support that older code and automated tests until you no longer support that older version.

As you think about how you handle versioning, consider the answer to questions like these:

- What happens to older versions?
- What happens to apps developed on older versions?
- Do new versions support all the functionality of the older apps, or must API customers need to update their apps to work with newer versions?
- Do you have a plan for minimizing the number of times you ask developers to upgrade or change versions?
- How many one-off versions are you prepared to create for "special" partners? What is the support cost associated with that decision?

The policy you develop for retiring or "sunsetting" old versions of your API will affect your versioning policy. You will have much happier API users if you have clear policies about how long an outdated version will be supported than if you provide only a week's notice that you are about to take down the old version or make a lot of changes. Expressing this sunsetting policy up front will inspire confidence and foster adoption.

It is important to note that policies around versioning will differ between public and private APIs. For public APIs, the developer community is presumably a large group of potentially unknown developers. Understanding their needs, expectations, and ability to adjust to your changes can be very difficult. For private APIs, however, the teams consuming the API are typically much closer, more inline with the changes to the API, more flexible, and often driving the need for advancement. Private API developers may not need long lead times for new versions. They may not even need multiple versions at all.

Having a Mediation Layer

Changing the API version does not have to be painful for users or hard on your systems. A technique called mediation can blunt some of the difficulties that come with necessary version changes. This is possible because, as we said earlier, APIs usually are based on self-describing data formats. Without any special code, a layer placed between the API client and the final API server can transform each request and response from the old version to the new without requiring any changes on the server.

How can you provide and manage different versions of the same API—or "mediate" (or transform) API content and syntax?

Alternatives include:

- Support multiple APIs (painful)
- Hold off the new version as long as possible and push customers to a one size fits all model (more painful)
- Create a mediation capability or layer that can transform between different shapes of the API, such as protocol, data, version, and credentials

Using a mediation layer, along with policy instead of business logic (as described in the next section) can ease your pain when it comes to versioning (and some other overarching issues, like security, rate limiting, and the like).

Although this is a useful technique, if the changes introduce new or changing response elements, mediation may not effectively insulate app developers from your changes.

Taking the Plunge: Going Versionless

As a practical matter, most APIs use versioning to protect API customers from an evolving API. (Developers dislike APIs that change all the time, and even some of the most famous ones do.) On the other hand, it can be very easy to get carried away with versioning, making support for a growing list of versions very difficult and time-consuming. For example, Netflix's API supports WiFi-enabled TVs that point to a very specific version of the Netflix API. That reference is sometimes baked into the firmware of the TV and is not able to change. Obviously, most people buy TVs to sit on their wall for 7-10 years. That means that the API to which that TV points must remain intact for the duration. As Netflix evolves the API, if it continues to spin out new versions on a yearly basis, the company could find itself supporting a dozen or more API versions! That kind of support model is untenable to maintain and will certainly result in many production outages.

Another approach is to strive to have your API be completely versionless. To achieve this, significant discipline and foresight is required.

Though difficult to achieve given the growing demands that most APIs face, it is possible and it is a worthy goal as it does have a range of benefits. A shared underlying system is preferable to a growing number of distinct but similar systems. This is particularly the case for APIs that are used by a large number of device partners, some of which may not be updatable, which means they may always point to the same version of an API.

NPR's Versionless API

The NPR API has been versionless since its inception in 2007 as a private API. It launched publicly in 2008 and has been versionless as well. All apps built on top of this API enjoy great stability and confidence that the API will continue to evolve without harming their apps.

There are a few key principles to keep in mind when considering this approach:

- Adding new features to an API typically does not require a new version. So, apply the principle "it is better to be incomplete than inaccurate." This principle suggests that you should withhold features from the API if you think there is a good chance that they will need to change.

- The design of your URIs and response formats should be generic where possible. For example, instead of outputting a field called home_phone_number, make the field phone_number and add an attribute that details the type (which, in this case, would be type="home"). This ensures that additions of new location phone numbers or the removal of the home phone number does not affect the design and structure of the API.

- There is a tendency to make the API a generic distribution pipe to satisfy the goals of all customers equally. This may make it difficult to maintain a stable API model, depending on the requirements of those using your API. If the burden of maintaining business logic for too many devices is too high, it might make sense to create custom API endpoints on a per-device (or even per request) basis, allowing them to be treated differently and allowing you to avoid needing to version the core API as you add new features to support a specific device.

- Generally, smaller developer communities that are very close to the API provider (such as internal mobile development teams) are much more resilient to a changing API. As a result, knowing your audience is critical when considering a versionless API. For an API like Google Maps, it is virtually impossible to make changes without versioning because of the huge number of unknown developers consuming it.

The benefit of a versionless API is that you don't have to support multiple versions of the system or ensure backward compatibility. The challenge of a versionless API is that it forces deeper considerations about adaptability upfront and may obligate you to make uncomfortable decisions, such as withholding functionality that could be useful. Supporting a versionless API is often easier to achieve with private than with public APIs.

Designing Infrastructure for APIs

This section focuses on design considerations related to infrastructure, including scalability, caching, and rate limiting.

How big should your API infrastructure be? The rule of thumb is "Design for the dream audience but provision for the expected load." Few API programs go from zero to 500 million daily requests overnight, and it's unwise to approach management with large budget requests unless there is a strong business case for that expense or strong evidence that the API will scale to justify that upfront cost. Even Twitter in its early days had many scaling problems (resulting in many outages), but the service was so compelling and unique that users put up with it while the system was unstable.

Data Center or Cloud?

A growing number of new websites and APIs run on a scalable cloud platform, most often Amazon EC2, where the size of the initial hardware order is irrelevant, because it can be scaled, up or down, quickly and as needed (sometimes dynamically, depending on how it's configured). Most API providers will do perfectly well running their system in the cloud. That said, most of the biggest APIs (such as Google, Yahoo!, and Facebook) run out of data centers and use hardware that they manage directly.

Some companies have established data centers and very specific requirements around latency or audit compliance that can be satisfied only by having physical access to the hardware the API runs on. Many API providers' biggest issue with latency has to do with the physical distance between server and customer, which is why some rely on content delivery networks (CDNs). Latency can also be addressed via caching.

Caching Strategies

From a systems perspective, faster is always better, and caching can reduce response times. If the API is slow, the apps that use it will be slow as well. If the apps are slow, end users are more likely to seek better, faster options. In the web world, one of the top reasons for people dropping a site is because of slow load times. The mobile world is no different. Caching is one way to mitigate some of these performance issues.

Keep in mind that today's API platforms are made of layers, and each layer has a cache. An API mediation layer can cache completed API responses close to the "edge of the network," an application server can have one caching tier for API responses and another to cache database results, and so on. CDNs like Akamai play a role as well; content APIs will often return a link to content that is, in turn, stored in a CDN.

Of course, depending on the content, the difficulty of caching varies. A weather page is easy to cache—forecasts rarely update more than once a minute. Twitter, on the other hand, is much more difficult to cache because every user views a different stream. Twitter's infrastructure has many layers of caching, which adjust dynamically to the nature of the content demanded—when Kanye West or Ashton Kutcher tweet, the cache is retained for a greater period because of the number of people requesting it, but timelines are unique for each individual.

Here are some general pieces of advice for API caching:

Measure first
> Your logging or API analytics infrastructure should tell you which are the most popular API calls and which are the slowest. The first targets for caching are the slowest, most frequently accessed API calls that return a result that doesn't change very often.

Don't forget invalidation
> The hardest part of caching is not deciding what to cache, but deciding how long to cache it and when it is invalid. You must plan and test this carefully—does content expire from the cache based on a timestamp in the response? Can there be a fixed time? Does one API call (such as a PUT or DELETE) invalidate the cache?

Watch it running
> An ineffective cache with a low hit rate does nothing for performance and might even make it worse.

AccuWeather's Experience with Global API Delivery

What are some of the issues that AccuWeather has encountered with global API delivery?

Localization. We offer the API in 37 different languages. We translate even down to the correct phraseology in the local market.

Performance and response time is important for global customers. We recently started doing over 1 billion API calls a day.

Caching considerations are important in global delivery, especially optimizing the cache for the right level of GPS detail; you don't need to go back to the data store for weather data at too fine a level of GPS detail.

The rules of the business are different in different regions. Our brand needs to translate appropriately in each market (for example, the preface "accu" might have different meanings in a local market.)

Support for international developers can also be a unique challenge. We do a lot of work to ensure our developer materials are equally clear to developers across different languages.

Chris Patti, Director of Technology, AccuWeather

Controlling API Traffic

Rate limiting is a control mechanism employed by API owners to prevent the system from being overtaxed by API data traffic and to tie API usage to specific business outcomes. There are various subcategories of rate limits, and in fact the whole topic is specifically tied to the general area of traffic management. We will cover all the options later in Chapter 8.

Before getting to the technical details, however, it is important to discuss how business-level rate limits, which we call *quotas*, affect the design of the API.

A quota is a rate limit that attaches a business outcome to a specific number of transactions. Its purpose is to maintain a business policy related to API usage. On Twitter, for example, application developers are allowed to check their timelines between 150 and 350 times an hour, depending on the current state of the Twitter infrastructure. Those who go over that quota receive an error. A common purpose for a quota is to divide developers into segments, each of which has a different quota, and thus a different relationship with the API. For example, it is common to offer API access with a small quota to any developer who signs up for an account, but require either additional verification, or even a charge, for a higher rate limit.

As with hardware and infrastructure, the need for a quota has a lot to do with scale and usage characteristics. The guiding question is, "How valuable is my information, and what happens if the API is enormously successful?" For example, some content APIs are fully open, require no user authentication, and thus need to be protected from too much traffic. Twitter has to have a rate limit because of the likelihood that users could check their timelines 1,000 times per second. The infrastructure can't absorb that level of traffic.

Clearly, it is possible to go overboard with quotas. Sometimes they are applied punitively, making the service almost unusable. It becomes difficult to test the service, and eventually developers move away from it. We encourage some flexibility—rates inevitably go higher when developers test their applications. A mechanism to charge developers for higher than normal rates can help manage those requests.

Don't forget that quotas have a benefit for private APIs too, even inside the corporate firewall, because they can help reduce risk. For instance, an organization may be considering opening up some of the enterprise "crown jewels" as an API to speed creation of future business products, but those "crown jewels" run on expensive and critical infrastructure. By deploying a quota, the team that owns the API has the option of making that content or service available for internal innovation, while reducing the risk of internal problems—and reducing the risk of an unpleasant meeting with the operations team! In other words, effective use of quotas can help an internal API team bring some of the agility of the Internet to the enterprise.

CHAPTER 6

API Security and User Management

Formulating effective API security is a critical design decision, as well as an ongoing operations imperative. This is an important subject, addressed in many books with a broader scope than ours. This chapter is by no means a definitive survey of Internet security techniques. Here we highlight the security issues and techniques that apply to designing and operating APIs specifically.

The security models you choose are an important characteristic of your API and must be appropriate for the business. If your API deals with sensitive finance data over public networks, stronger security measures will be required than if your API simply passes data around for a private audience on a protected network.

The operative questions for designing your API security framework include:

- What assets are you trying to secure? How much security do you need to secure them?
- How will the security measures you plan to implement impact performance of the API? Will it complicate programming against it?
- Who is using the API? Do you need users to identify themselves before they use applications built using the API?
- Is it OK if they just identify the application that is running and not the person who is using it?

Very few API providers offer APIs without some form of identification, such as registration for using the API. Most APIs employ one or more of these basic security techniques:

Identification
Who is making an API request?

Authentication
Are they really who they say they are?

Authorization
Are they allowed to do what they are trying to do?

Do you need all three? Perhaps not. Some APIs only need to establish identity and don't really need authentication or fine-grained authorization; it all depends on what is on the other end of that API. The following sections summarize some approaches to API security.

User Management

Good user management can pay off by reducing support costs and increasing customer satisfaction. This includes setting developers up with an account and any authentication credentials they need to work with your API. But at least for public APIs, you'll also need a user interface (UI), and all API types will need processes to add, reset, revoke, or delete these accounts. You may also need to take into account how to hand out API keys or OAuth tokens, and even consider an approval process, if you choose to go that route.

Also, consider whether you can make things simpler by defining rights around standard user profiles. For example, gold customers may have access to certain APIs or requests that bronze customers do not.

Finally, consider any other information you can give developers, such as usage statistics and alerts on versioning upgrades and outages, that make it faster and easier to work with you—ideally, you will answer their questions without requiring them to call you.

Do You Need to Start from Scratch?

Before building or buying a user management interface, consider whether you might be able to extend some other existing user management UI and processes to work for developers requesting access to your API.

For example, a public website implemented by Apigee built its own user management system quickly, using an existing Salesforce.com account, with just a couple of integration points added to the account provisioning functionality. The key question that drives this decision is: How much integration do you need into your existing business processes? For example, do you need to create accounts in your CRM system and make sure you have enough developer information to map developers to applications and customers?

Questions to Ask About User Management

For onboarding developers:

- Do you already have a way to manage user accounts to reuse for your API? Do you also wish to offer OAuth keys?
- If you have no user management at all, what does a user need to do in order to sign up to use your API?

- Can users sign up quickly and easily using a web browser? Should they be able to?
- Can you simplify things by defining tiers of users?
- What kind of information do they need to access?

For maintaining and managing accounts:

- Can you reset user passwords?
- What user interface do you want to create for user management?
- Can users manage their accounts using a website, or is there some other way?
- Can you monitor their usage? Can they monitor it themselves?
- Can you revoke user accounts?
- Do you need to implement an approval or screening process?
- Do you need reporting and analytics around users—active developers, engagement, and retention rates?

Integrating your API users into the rest of your business:

- Does developer activity need to get mapped into sales, support, and ERP systems?
- Does your API key structure enable you to map developers to applications, your customers, and their end users?
- Does user data need to be integrated with existing profiles or user data systems? Can you use existing SSO (single sign-on) systems?
- Can you create usage incentives by providing developers access to their own usage data?

Identification

One of the first steps to ensuring that your API is protected from unauthorized use is to determine who is using it. One common method that allows an API to determine which applications are using it (and in turn which developers build them) is by using an *API key*.

API keys originated with the first public web services, such as the Yahoo! and Google APIs. The publishers wanted to have some way to establish identity of calling applications without the complexity of passwords. API keys are simple, random identifiers that the developer usually passes via an HTTP query parameter or something equally simple—thus, they are easy to include in every API request.

In order for a developer to build an application with an API, the developer must obtain a unique key and send it with every API request. So, API keys help the API provider monitor which applications are using the API. Through API keys, the developer can also gain visibility into how his application is being used since request metrics are often collected based on the API key. From an identification perspective, API keys are a powerful and compelling choice because of the analytics data they can reveal to the API publisher and to the developer.

API keys are deliberately simple to hand out and include—they are often not encrypted or signed, so they could potentially be discovered by an attacker. For this reason, API keys are more of an auditing tool than a security measure, but for some APIs, this type of identification is all that is needed.

While the API key is not an authentication tool, it can serve a different security function. It can be the method for turning off access for rogue applications that (intentionally or otherwise) flood the system with calls, whether inadvertently flooding because of programming mistakes, launching a distributed denial of service attack, breaching terms of use, or practicing any other form of abuse. Filtering or blocking traffic with a certain API key effectively turns off access for any such application.

Once an app gains access to the API, it is wise to ask for authentication from the API's end user if an API makes extensive use of personal information—Facebook, for example, certainly needs to allow the users to control what parts of their personal data are exposed to third parties. But many other popular APIs do not require user sign-in, including Google Maps and Yahoo! Maps. In general, it's best if you can find a way to err on the side of openness and take a little bit of risk.

Authentication: Proving Who You Are

Authentication methods determine whether someone accessing an API is really who they say they are. Authentication methods include usernames and passwords, methods more common in the corporate world (SAML, X.509), and an important method in use by many APIs today: OAuth.

Usernames and Passwords

With more sensitive data, an API key is not enough. Typically, API keys are hard-coded into the source code of mobile apps and may be sent in clear text over the network with no encryption. That's fine when they're used for auditing and analytics, but since the compromise of one API key could affect millions of devices, they're not adequate for authentication when sensitive data is involved. An alternative is username/password authentication, which is the authentication scheme supported by many secure websites.

It's easiest to use HTTP Basic authentication, which most websites use and which nearly all clients and servers support. There is no special processing required, as long as the caller takes reasonable precautions to keep the password secret, and as long as SSL is used for all communications so that no eavesdropper can discover the secret.

Usernames and passwords also work well for application-to-application communications. The only obstacle, from the client's perspective, is storing the password securely

---

—if there is any possibility of an attacker reading the file where the password is stored, it must be encrypted in some way. If that password is being used by a server, where should you store it? If you are running an application server that uses a database, you already solved this problem because the database usually requires a password too and is likely only directly accessible inside a firewall. The more sophisticated application server platforms include a credential mapper that can be used to store such passwords relatively securely.

Session-Based Authentication

Lots of early APIs supported session-based authentication. In these schemes, the user first has to call a "login" method, which takes the username and password as the input, and returns a unique session key. The user must include the session key in each request, and call "logout" when he is done. This way, authentication is kept to a single pair of API calls, and everything else is based on the session.

In its early instantiation, cookie-based authentication was cumbersome because it required client-side programmers to keep track of state and put additional burdens on server-side infrastructure.

In some scenarios, however, cookie-based authentication is not as cumbersome, particularly in private APIs where the API provider also has control over the clients that access it. In those scenarios, where the number of clients is limited and known, using a cookie to help start the session by authenticating the user can be very effective (as long as the clients are all web-based). After the session is started, however, and the user is authenticated, the statefulness of this approach ends. All subsequent requests are stateless, passing the authenticated consumer keys to the API.

Netflix is currently moving toward cookie-based authentication for device implementations. The process works like this. The session start command grabs the cookie values, hits the server to authenticate, then passes forward only the information needed for each request. This allows Netflix to maintain a relatively "stateless" API but the cookie is stateful and helps authenticate the user for all subsequent requests and sessions. This approach may be applicable to other companies, but it will depend on the level of control of the client apps and the nature of the API itself.

Other Authentication Methods

Once we leave the world of plain HTTP, we encounter many other methods of authentication, including SAML (Security Assertion Markup Language), X.509 certificates, and two-way SSL (Secure Sockets Layer), which are based on secure distribution of public keys to individual clients, as well as various WS-Security specifications, which build on SOAP to provide a variety of services.

An API primarily used by enterprise customers—that is, big IT organizations—might consider authentication mechanisms such as X.509 certificates or SAML because they provide stronger authentication than a simple username/password combination. Also, a large enterprise may have an easier time accessing an API written to the SOAP standard because enterprise developers often use tools that can import a WSDL file and generate an API client in a few minutes.

Like many things in the world of APIs, it is a question of the audience. Enterprise developers with enterprise tools will understand SAML and perhaps even be required to use it. Most other developers will not.

OAuth

OAuth is an open protocol for allowing secure API authorization from desktop and web applications through a simple and standard method. It manages handshakes between applications and is used when an API publisher wants to know who is communicating with the system. Many of the largest API publishers have implemented OAuth to handle write access to their APIs.

An example of OAuth lies in the relationships between social networking sites such as Facebook and Flickr. Let's say a user wants to get some pictures out of Flickr and post them to Facebook, but may not want to type her Flickr password into Facebook. Before the arrival of OAuth, most APIs supported HTTP Basic authentication. Under HTTP Basic, Facebook would need to store the user's Flickr password somewhere. This causes a problem for the user, who now must trust Facebook with her password, which potentially presents an even larger problem if she ever wishes to change her password, since it is now stored by many different websites.

Rather than relying on a single password as the master key for every application that accesses an API, OAuth creates a token, similar to a valet key for a car. An OAuth token gives *one* application access to *one* API on behalf of *one* user. By contrast, a password gives *every* application access to *anything* that password can unlock. This is dangerous, as many people use the same password for multiple applications and websites.

In another scenario, mobile phone users can access applications without having to reenter their passwords each time. The phone stores an OAuth token rather than a password. If the phone is stolen, the thief cannot uncover the password, only the token, which can be set to expire after a certain amount of time.

Because it relies on security tokens rather than shared passwords, OAuth makes APIs more resilient to security breaches. For instance, in the case above, a user may discover that her Facebook password has been compromised. If all the applications that she uses access Facebook through OAuth, then she can change her Facebook password without worrying about breaking all her apps.

Furthermore, the different versions and options of the OAuth standard support a variety of ways for API clients to authenticate themselves. The simplest is a "bearer token," which is a large random number that is transmitted with each request and encrypted using SSL.

OAuth also supports a signature option, which uses both a token and a secret. When a request is sent over the network containing an OAuth signature, the data in the token is encrypted using the token secret, but the secret itself is never sent over the network. That way, regardless of whether SSL is in use, there is no way to gain access to the token secret by sniffing the network. This makes it a good choice for APIs that handle large amounts of non-sensitive data, as they can avoid the overhead of SSL while keeping the user credentials secure from eavesdropping.

In order for the OAuth handshake to work, each application that uses an API needs a set of credentials similar to the "API key" that we discussed above. This gives the API provider an opportunity to control access to the API by particular applications as well. For instance, if Flickr is compromised and it is crucially important to keep the site secure, the Facebook administrators have the option of revoking Flickr's OAuth credentials, thus cutting off access for all users.

OAuth has become a necessity for organizations that have APIs associated with websites or mobile applications that require passwords.

Like any security scheme, there is a significant caretaking requirement on the server side for API operations. It is important that, as a part of securing the server side of the API, OAuth tokens be protected from unauthorized access. Just like your password database, the compromise of an entire database of OAuth tokens would be catastrophic.

The specifics of how best to protect OAuth tokens depend on how they are used. For instance, if bearer tokens are used, they should be encrypted on the server side via a one-way hash. Or, if signatures are used, the tokens and secrets must be readable by the server or the protocol does not work, so they need to be encrypted using field-level database encryption. As the technology changes, other requirements will emerge—the only constant is care and vigilance.

Fortify Authentication with SSL

With the increasing importance of mobile computing, both over cellular networks and from public WiFi access points, the need to encrypt Internet traffic is greater than it was in the days when most critical transactions occurred between one large corporate network and another. Eavesdropping is a real possibility today, and for that reason every API that deals with sensitive information must support, or indeed *require*, the use of SSL to ensure that all traffic is securely encrypted from the end-user device to the API endpoint.

The cost of doing this, however, is highly variable. Once an SSL connection is set up, it doesn't add that much processing overhead. However, setting up the connection involves multiple round-trips, which add latency and expensive public-key cryptographic functions. With the rise of mobile computing, an API that performs well with

SSL during benchmarks on the local network may perform much worse when accessed by a mobile phone.

The bottom line is that SSL is required in two cases—when sensitive data is transmitted, and when the specific authentication mechanism requires it.

In the second case, it is important to note that OAuth authentication using bearer tokens, HTTP Basic authentication, and some other authentication mechanisms are reliant on SSL to keep keys secure—otherwise an eavesdropper can easily see the users' password or token. However, when OAuth is used with a signature rather than a bearer token, it is possible to keep the token and secret secure without relying on SSL.

It is important to consider the sensitivity of the various types of data that your API will offer. Don't rule out the possibility of having some requests, such as end-user registration, go through SSL while others, such as retrieving a posted comment, may not need to.

Identification vs. Authentication: Google Maps vs. Twitter

The Yahoo and Google Maps APIs are fairly open. These APIs ask who you are, but aren't concerned with what address you are looking up. They use an API key to establish identity, but don't authenticate or authorize. If you use someone else's API key, it's not recommended, but it is not a serious security breach because the data and functionality exposed are not particularly sensitive.

The API key lets the API provider identify who is making an API call so that they can limit the number of requests that users can make. Identity is important for the mapping APIs because widely used services need to keep traffic volume under control.

Twitter's API, by contrast, is open for looking up public information about a user, but some operations require authentication. Twitter requires that all API clients authenticate using OAuth. Twitter also has authorization checks in its code so that users cannot tweet on behalf of another user without the other user's OAuth key. This is an example of an API that implements OAuth for both authentication and authorization.

Encryption

The data protection imperative for API operations is to guard against data breaches. No one ever wants accidental customer data exposure through their APIs. In addition to managing identity, authentication, and authorization, another important aspect of API management is data protection—specifically encryption.

First things first—protecting sensitive data requires knowing what the data is, where it is, and how sensitive it is to you and your customers. Be aware of the various regulations and best practices for Social Security numbers, credit card numbers, home addresses, birthdays, and other sensitive data.

Once you have identified which data is sensitive, you can think about how to best protect it in your API.

Encryption must be part of any API with sensitive data. Many of the social networking sites now use SSL encryption, although this was initially thought to be unnecessary. The vulnerability of wireless traffic on public networks, and the propensity of Twitter and Facebook users to sit in cafés, where they would be vulnerable to sniffing attacks, changed this paradigm. The contemporary security discussion assumes encryption by default; recently, the conversation has switched from "Why do we need encryption?" to "Why wouldn't we need encryption?"

For most APIs, the most critical encryption mechanism is SSL, as discussed earlier in this chapter. It works on every platform. Using SSL to encrypt any sensitive data is the least your API should do. Another alternative is to encrypt either all or part of each message using XML Encryption. (This is a W3C standard implemented by many SOA products.) However, this requires you and your clients to manage public/private key pairs, so deploying this technology can be complex, and it has a larger performance impact. However, XML Encryption is tremendously useful when it's important to manage sensitive data behind the API. An example scenario would be a situation when API data must not only be transmitted securely over the Internet, but also stored in internal systems in encrypted form, on a disk or in a database. Otherwise, stick with SSL.

Threat Detection and Prevention

Any server that receives data over the Internet is subject to attack. Some attacks are more easily targeted at an API and merit additional consideration.

SQL Injection

SQL injection takes advantage of internal systems that construct database queries using string concatenation. If there's a way to take data from the client and paste it inside a database query, there may be a way to compromise the system using SQL injection. The best way to prevent SQL injection is to code the backend systems to make SQL injection impossible. Since it is not possible to prove with 100 percent certainty that all the programming is correct, it's also important to stop SQL injection attempts before they get to backend systems.

For example, an API gateway can be inserted between the client and the servers running the API that scans all incoming traffic, or certain input fields, for regular expression patterns that denote a possible SQL injection attempt. In other words, Joe Smith may be a valid name, but `DELETE * FROM CUSTOMERS` is not!

SQL injections are real and they have been part of a number of well-publicized security incidents. Any API that accepts input that might be inserted into an SQL database for later use must protect itself.

XML and JSON Attacks

Most APIs, and all transactional APIs, accept PUT and POST requests from clients containing data that is usually formatted in XML or JSON. Any API that accepts either XML or JSON from untrusted resources can be subject to attacks, just as any server is potentially vulnerable to any file that is uploaded from a non-trusted source. Validating XML and JSON documents for these kinds of problems—or just ensuring that they are actually XML or JSON in the first place—is essential.

XML and JSON attacks take advantage of the flexibility of these data formats by constructing a document that could cause a problem for a backend system, such as causing the software to try to allocate more memory than is available. One common attack method is to generate a document that is nested many levels deep, or with extremely large field names or comments.

These attacks aren't always intentional. If you have ever used an API such as StAX to construct an XML document, but forgotten to add all the end tags, you can create an invalid XML document. APIs are potentially more vulnerable to these mistakes even more than they are vulnerable to malicious attacks.

However, well-documented XML attacks of all varieties have been described on the Internet for years, and may be used maliciously. They range from the simple attacks that we describe above, to complex ones that take advantage of the older "DTD" mechanism that was used to describe the structure of XML documents. And just because JSON is newer and less complicated doesn't mean that there aren't ways to create malformed and dangerous JSON documents as well.

Data Masking

Data masking is the practice of preventing inadvertent data exposure in API responses.

Encryption is critical to keeping sensitive data private, but in some cases, it may make sense to try to reuse internal services and data and expose them via the API. However, to keep sensitive data private in such a case, you might need to screen—or mask—some private data for the API. This means using an XML or JSON transformation to either remove or obfuscate certain data in an API response. While this technique must be used with care, there may be cases in which only certain API users are authorized to see certain information. For example, there might be an API call that returns a user record with all the details when the user herself calls the API, but only limited data when a customer service representative accesses the user record using the API.

In the latter case, you could implement data masking by building only one version of the API on a backend server and adding a data transformation rule that removes the user's home address, if the request is coming from a customer service representative's account. If you have many services, you might consider having a common layer that performs these types of transformations—especially if you need to add certain data fields as well as masking fields.

General Recommendations

The next two sections summarize general recommendations for API data protection and API security in general.

API Data Protection Recommendations

Use SSL when the API includes sensitive data, or if the authentication mechanism does not include an encryption component. HTTP Basic authentication and OAuth with bearer tokens, for instance, allow an eavesdropper to intercept the security credentials unless SSL is used.

Always defend against injection attacks, in the backend server, at the edge of the network, or both.

If your API accepts incoming parameters via HTTP POST or some other method, you must defend against many types of data attacks. These include large inputs, payloads or attachments, header bombs, replay attacks, message tampering and more.

Consider using data masking in a common transformation layer if your backend servers return some data that should not be given out to all users of the API.

For writable APIs, don't simply rely on IP addresses to secure your APIs. IP addresses can be spoofed, are not always unique, and can't be trusted as a single authentication scheme. A combination of approaches works best.

API Security Recommendations

Use API keys only for nonsensitive, read-only data. If you have a public API—which exposes data you'd make public on the Internet anyway—consider issuing nonsensitive API keys. These are easy to implement and still give you a way to identify applications and developers. Armed with an API key, you have the option of establishing a quota for your API, or at least monitoring usage by application. Without one, the only way to track usage is through IP addresses, which are not reliable. For example, the Yahoo Maps Geocoding API issues API keys so it can track its users and establish a quota, but the data that it returns is not sensitive, so it's not critical to keep the key secret.

Public APIs should use OAuth 2.0 for APIs that are intended for use by native and mobile apps. The advantage of using an OAuth token rather than a password is also important for mobile apps, to ensure that a user's password is not propagated to every app and device that they use. Typically, authenticating to OAuth requires that the user enter her password into a web browser screen, rather than the application itself. That means that the application never actually sees the user's password. This adds a layer of security when an API is used by mobile apps built by untrusted developers for a public API. OAuth also has the ability to allow the API provider to revoke tokens for an individual user, or for an entire application, without requiring the user to change his or her original password. This is critical if a mobile device is compromised or if a rogue application is discovered.

Private APIs should consider OAuth 2.0 for native and mobile apps. Private API providers have control over the clients that are built for the API, so it is safer to allow the application to collect the user's password directly. However, OAuth still makes it possible for the application to acquire a token, store it on the device, and immediately discard the password, which reduces the risk that the password will be compromised.

Support other types of authentication for server-to-server APIs. Two-way SSL, SAML, and even usernames combined with long, random passwords are fine security schemes that have the advantage of being well supported by client and server platforms. For an API that is only used by a small number of internal or partner systems, and which is used by servers and not by end users who have passwords, OAuth works but it is overkill.

Use SSL for everything sensitive (or maybe even for everything). Unless your API exclusively has open and nonsensitive data, support SSL and consider enforcing it by redirecting any API traffic on the non-SSL port to the SSL port. It makes other authentication schemes more secure, and keeps your user's private API data from prying eyes—and it's not all that hard to do.

Sanitize incoming and outgoing data. This will prevent malicious code or content from entering your system or being executed by clients that read your data. This practice should be employed for all APIs, but may be especially important for writable ones. For example, for a writable API, you do not want to allow insertion of JavaScript that could be used for cross-site scripting attacks when users visit your website. For example, if a parameter value is known to be numeric, it should be validated as numeric before being passed. Again, this practice should be applied for all APIs, but may be more needed for writable APIs.

CHAPTER 7

Legal Considerations for Your API Strategy

There are two major types of legal considerations when developing an API: What are your rights for distributing the content to others and what are the rights that you want to grant to others who want to consume from your API? The former question is associated with legal rights and contractual relationships between your company and others. The latter is typically handled through direct contracts with partners or Terms of Use contracts for the public.

Particularly for content-related APIs, the rights and legal considerations for distributing content must be considered before developing your API. Before starting, here are some fundamental questions to answer:

- What rights do you have to the content that you provide in the API?
- What rights can you or do you want to grant the consumers of the API?
- Are different levels of access needed for different API audiences?
- Have all the legal considerations been taken into account? If not, a "soft launch" or beta period may be necessary, amounting to private testing of rights scenarios.
- Are you taking into account other parts of the organization or systems that could impact the rights management for the API?

Who owns the rights?

Not understanding the ownership of the content that you are publishing in a public or private API can get you in big trouble. Sports scores, market data, and a wide variety of other information that you acquire is in fact "owned" by someone else and distributing it without having the rights to do so can have serious implications.

To give your audience the best experience possible, the experience they expect, do your best to renegotiate existing contracts to free up the content for redistribution.

Rights Management

Rights management—the capability and permission of an API provider to repurpose content it does not own—can be a thorny issue, and the resolution of policy around this issue needs to be embedded in the API in a sophisticated way, both technically and from a business perspective. There can be a highly nuanced technical implementation involved, as circumstances for each content producer will be variable.

In Practice: Rights Management at NPR

NPR's experience provides a useful example of how an API provider dealt with complex rights management issues.

Because NPR distributes content to four distinct audiences, some of which have unknown destinations, it is critical to make sure the API itself can control what is offered and to whom. To handle these kinds of issues, NPR built a permissions and rights management system into the API. But that was not enough. Rights management starts with drawing up contracts and ensuring that content is tagged appropriately. Without these key steps, the rights management system cannot accurately withhold content that is prohibited for distribution. NPR took the following steps to create its rights management system.

Contracts

Before launching the API, NPR consulted with its legal team, reviewing existing contracts and its rights tagging system. NPR acquires content from other public radio organizations, such as *Fresh Air* from WHYY and the radio series *StoryCorps*. The contracts for this content allowed for limited digital distribution, but not through the API.

This highlights two points. First, at launch, NPR needed to incorporate a rights management system in the API that could identify specific types of content, then restrict that content from being distributed in certain ways to certain types of users. The second key point is that NPR has been shifting its contract strategy to enable more content to be distributable anywhere NPR content appears, including through its API. Shortly after launch, the *Fresh Air* and *StoryCorps* contracts were modified and the content was able to surface in full through the API.

Rights Tagging System

NPR has a rights tagging process within its content management system, through which the editorial staff identifies content that it cannot redistribute. This is critical for the success of rights management, because if you cannot identify content correctly, you can't restrict its use. A sizable portion of this system involves manual effort because it relates to editorial judgment in selecting content from external sources. Editorial staffers enter the assets into NPR's content management system, which contains appropriate fields for tagging the owner of the content.

Some feeds, such as AP Business, are automated; such stories and assets are assembled through automated systems and are tagged by scripts.

There are also scripts for removing content from the system based on contractual obligations. For example, if NPR has the rights to present an image for only 30 days, scripts purge the system of that image and its metadata at the appropriate time.

Rights Management System

Once content has been tagged, it enters a rights management system, which has four aspects:

- Query-level filtering
- Story-level filtering
- Asset-level filtering
- User permissions

Query-level filtering enables the API to remove any story or "list" (that is, topic, program, series, and so on) from being delivered to specific users due to restrictions in contractual rights for redistribution. For example, prior to the renegotiation of the *Fresh Air* contract, the query-level filter would restrict access to that content for specific users.

After the *Fresh Air* contract was renegotiated, this content became available to all audiences. At that point, the API would return stories in a list when *Fresh Air* was requested. At this point, the next level of restriction, the *story-level filter*, gets applied. This filter determines which stories need to be removed before returning the response to the user. For example, if the user were not authorized to see stories that belong to other companies, that story would be pruned out of the results even though it otherwise would normally be returned by such a query. If one of those stories is among the top ten stories of the day, the system will skip over that story in a user request for the top 10 stories and substitute the 11th story for the 10th.

Asset-level filtering is less stringent than story-level filtering because it does not remove the story completely. Rather, it displays the story but removes any assets that the user does not have the rights to see. For example, if a given *Fresh Air* story has an AP image attached to it, the asset-level filtering will remove that image when returning the rest of the story to specific API users.

The final element of this system is *permissions*. When the API launched, NPR's permission levels included Public, Partner, Station, and NPR.org, with access privileges that increase in that order. For each level, a distinct list of IDs is associated with each filter type. As a result, the same story in the NPR system can theoretically be removed for the Public user, present only RSS content for Partner users, present everything but images for Stations, and be fully available to the NPR.org users. Meanwhile, a different story could theoretically have a completely different permission scheme, enabling NPR.org users no access to it while public users can see it all.

Figure 7-1 shows how this filtering layer sits on top of NPR's content management system.

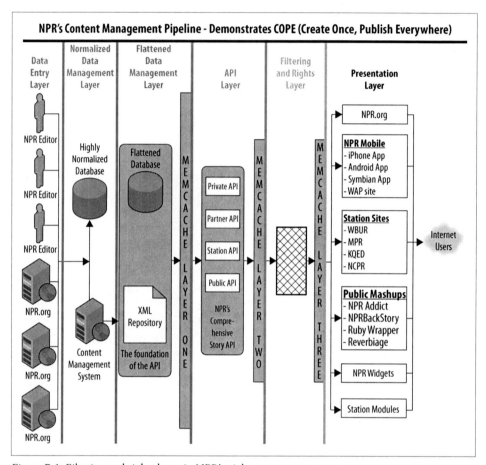

Figure 7-1. Filtering and rights layer in NPR's rights management system

Contracts and Terms of Use

The terms of use for an API differ across the target audiences for those APIs. A public API and private API will have different contracts governing their relationships with users. Public API developers are subject to whatever is in the public terms of use. For private API use, any contractual agreement supersedes that of the public terms of use. And in the case of a private API that is used by internal development teams, the agreement is more operational than contractual.

Within the terms of use, it is also important to incorporate any trademarks, copyrights, and branding requirements. For example, the Twitter API restricts the API consumer from using "Twitter" as the name of an iPhone app. That name is reserved for the company itself.

Unlike APIs, terms of use are versioned and may change often as your API, company, and even legal team changes. While your API may not be versioned, the API infrastructure must be able to support changes to terms of use, as they are deemed necessary.

Terms of use are often directed at the end user of the API as well as at the developers who build applications using the API. When they are directed at the end user, the API infrastructure must include a mechanism to prevent API access until a particular end user has consented to the terms of use. Furthermore, when the terms of use change, the API infrastructure must ensure that the user consents to the new terms before letting them continue, and so on and so forth.

This sort of mechanism works well when combined with the token-based security model of OAuth. In order to obtain an OAuth token, users usually provide their security credentials to the API provider using a web-based form. This login form, which may actually be a complex application with multiple pages that follows the OAuth specification, can ask the user for consent and not allow the login to succeed until it is granted. When the terms of service change, the API provider can revoke the OAuth tokens, causing them to automatically go through the authentication process, including granting consent, again. If your company has terms of use for your website, it is important to incorporate the API terms into the overarching terms applied for the site and/or other digital properties.

Privacy Policies

Privacy policies come into play if and when your company handles sensitive or personal data. It is critical to ensure that your API takes into account your company's overarching privacy policies. This could mean that the API program adopts established privacy policies used in other areas of the company. More likely, you will probably need to modify your policies to cover the growing needs that the API creates. For example, if the privacy policy for your website ensures that any user data will only be used on your website, then if you plan to use the API for your mobile strategy, it is likely that you will need to broaden the policy to allow the user data to be used on all of your branded digital properties. On the other hand, if you plan to offer a public API, it is possible that such user data will need to be restricted to the public audience. As a result, the privacy policy won't need to change, as the offering will simply adhere to existing policies.

Data Retention Policies

Data retention is an important aspect of the API's overall terms of use and policy structure. Such policies vary greatly depending on the API provider's industry, business model, and API offering. These policies are designed to ensure that applications and data that are used from the API do not grow stale, misrepresent your company, or potentially compromise you or your users.

For example, Facebook has a 24-hour data retention policy, meaning that developers are to retain user data 24 hours or less. Facebook wants to restrict retention to a relatively narrow window because its users are active in updating their personal content. Moreover, Facebook also wants to ensure a tight window of time that this user data can be used to provide some degree of protection for their users.

Meanwhile NPR disallows retention beyond a period of time any longer than what is needed to create a "good content experience." The data that NPR offers is not particularly sensitive from a user perspective, but timeliness and accuracy of news and cultural content is an important part of the branding and news experience. A longer retention policy could result in apps or sites presenting NPR news content many days after it is relevant. Moreover, it is important to not provide NPR users with the ability to create a duplicate NPR.org site and the data retention policy helps enforce that prohibition.

It is important to recognize the sensitivity of the various pieces of content that you plan to offer in the API. Some of the content may have stricter retention policies than others and it is fair to apply different terms for different content. For example, Netflix has a 24-hour retention policy for most content, but a 1-year policy for credentials needed for a user to log in to an app.

Attribution of Content and Branding

Another key aspect of the overall policy structure is attribution for content, particularly as it applies to content APIs. One of the key business drivers for many companies is brand awareness. When a content API is offered to external parties, the API provider must ensure that branding is protected for each content producer represented in the API. The external parties must also understand how you want your brand to be handled. This is a key concern for AccuWeather. "When you build an API, you have to consider how it will be used. You need to help developers use your API and your brand correctly. We can't stress this point enough," said Steve Smith, CIO.

It behooves API owners to write attribution requirements into terms of service to ensure that third-party developers or companies using the API and its associated data adequately attribute the content to the API owner as the source of that information through a copyright symbol, logo, or the like. Although terms of service represent one way to enforce attribution, it is also sensible to enforce attribution by embedding it in appropriate fields in the delivered content.

Responding to Misuse

In the vast majority of cases, users of your API do not intend to misuse content or services. As a result, if you encounter misuse, it is best to try to understand the intent of the API consumer. In our experience, approaching the offending API consumer and explaining where the breach occurred is typically enough to resolve the matter. After all, if the developer is interested enough in your company and API to spend time, effort, and money on developing something on top of it, they will very likely be equally interested in accommodating your requests.

In the rare case when you encounter bad intent, it is important to have a response plan in place that answers the following questions:

- Who is responsible for assessing the misuse?
- Who is responsible for contacting the API consumer?
- If the problem persists, what are the legal implications?
- Who terminates access for the API consumer? When? Under what conditions?

Finally, keep in mind that if you know about misuse and do not respond to it, you may be in a weakened legal position if you choose to take action later. Your inaction in the face of known misuse may be considered "implied consent."

CHAPTER 8

Operating and Managing an API

The best API design in the world falls flat if the experience of the people who use the implementation is substandard. In a sense, operations is really about making sure that users of the API have a positive experience and are happy with the API's performance. This positive experience will ultimately carry on to your end users, generating greater value to your business.

APIs start with a set of processes and an organizational structure for delivering a good experience, including a customer service plan and communications plan. In other words, operations is not only about technology—it's also about support and communication. These apply to all audiences of the API, whether private or public.

Without a reliable operating model, an API will fail to deliver on its promises. Without appropriate management and monitoring capabilities, it is impossible to administer and learn from an API. This chapter walks you through some of the guidelines we have used for making the ongoing operation of an API smooth and successful.

Operating an API

If you are already familiar with operating a website, then operating an API will seem familiar. Customers are located all over the world, in different time zones, and they usually choose to interact with your product when you're not at work.

On the other hand, if you operate internal IT systems such as ERP or CRM, an API may seem like a whole new world. The focus of operations is typically on keeping the API running 24/7 with little or no scheduled downtime and on carefully deploying traffic management policies to ensure that some users don't cause operational problems for other users.

In general, the operations people on your API team need to be ready for a bevy of possible questions, including:

- For each audience, what are your service-level agreements (SLAs) for outages, and what are the expected response times for your support staff?

- What are your SLAs for error rates, latencies, and other performance-based metrics?
- What monitoring system do you have? Who is alerted, in what order, if the API goes down? What are the escalation policies?
- Who should the customers contact? Who's responsible for responding? How soon? Do you have different contact rules for different audiences?
- How do you get feedback about your product? If you are running a public portal, do you use a platform such as GetSatisfaction?
- What is your communication plan for proactively reporting problems and managing expectations?
- What happens if there's "too much good news"? What happens if TechCrunch or Hacker News writes an article about you, and your volume increases by a factor of 10 or 100 in a matter of hours?
- What kind of failover and disaster recovery procedures do you have in place if key servers go down?

Operational Information on Demand: The API Status Page

The industry has evolved to a new standard for providing operational information about APIs. An API status page is a special webpage that is supported on different technical infrastructure than the main API and whose only function is to let users know what's going on with the API at a technical level at any time they choose to have a look. Twitter follows this practice (see Figure 8-1), as do many other popular APIs. This has particular utility for public APIs, but may be equally valuable for internal API users as well. (By hosting the status page on a different technical infrastructure, you prevent the rather obvious problem of not being able to provide users with the status of the API because the API is down!)

Another recent industry best practice is to use microblogging or social media services such as Twitter to report on status. If there is indeed a major problem with your infrastructure, it's likely that someone will "tweet" about it, and in a negative way. By proactively informing your community of your status using those same tools, you don't fix the problem but you do keep your community informed, which goes a long way towards ensuring good will and happy users.

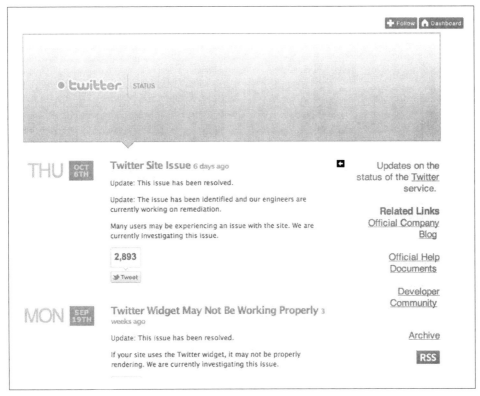

Figure 8-1. Twitter status page

Handling Ops Issues

API providers may not think through all of the issues related to operations. Jason Sirota of XO Group Inc., formerly known as The Knot Inc., says, "An API is not just a development effort; it's just as much as an ops effort (if not moreso). Ops issues need to be identified and addressed at the beginning."

Providing a test environment for customers is another best practice, according to Tim Madewell of Innotas. "If you're going to have customers build against your API, you need a process to check, verify, and certify what they are doing. Give the customer a test environment and then tell operations that a customer is going into production. You can put new customer deployments in a 'probationary' environment if need be."

As you're monitoring activity on the API, consider what's acceptable by starting with simply monitoring and sampling what a typical profile or footprint of an API user looks like. "What does an API user look like?" asks Madewell. "For example, should I allow a return of more than x megabytes per call, or should I allow more than x number of calls per hour?" Ops planning, monitoring, and testing against the original API assumptions are important parts of offering an API and understanding the profile of a typical API user.

Service-Level Agreements

Service-level agreements (SLAs) are used in different ways, depending upon the business context of the API. For public APIs, contractual SLAs are typically quite weak; they usually amount to a substantial effort to make sure that operational performance (in terms of uptime and latencies) is excellent, coupled with very weak promises about service levels and or remedies. For more specific business arrangements, the SLAs can be much stronger. In any event, strong operational performance, which is the reality of the SLA, will always need to be there, or users will vote with their feet. No contractual SLA can make up for poor performance. In some ways, the non-contractual, "operational" SLA is like a common-law marriage. The trust and track record have to be there, even if the legal "teeth" are absent.

When there is money on the line, on the other hand, failing to meet the SLA has greater consequences. The contract needs to include explicit documentation of remedies for outages, interruptions of service, security events, and the like. Ultimately, however, these remedies are not what the consumer of the API is looking for—they would much rather have excellent service with little or no downtime.

If your API depends on other Internet or external services, it is important to factor into your thinking the SLAs that they have with you. For example, if you know that you are dependent on three internal services, each of which have a latency SLA of about 100ms, then your SLA to your API developers should be no less than 300ms simply by the fact that your dependencies will not guarantee better than that. Of course, your SLA also needs to include whatever latencies your processing will incur, so you would need to add that on top of the 300ms as well.

Issue Management

Inevitably, your API will have the occasional bug or operational issue, and you will need a system for developers to log issues, whether they are internal or external. A simple page that allows a dialogue between users and the API owner's operations teams can go a long way toward resolving issues quickly and keeping application makers happy. Reporting can be automated, in a similar fashion to the crash reports Microsoft includes with its applications, or manual, which can work as a suggestion box, as well as a troubleshooting forum.

Issue management can also be a forum for proactive communication. Although it's not always possible for larger companies, the more direct interaction you can have with a developer who is having a problem, the better. At the very least, the issue management facility of your API should make it easy for developers to log an issue and know what to expect in terms of when and how it will be resolved.

Operational Monitoring and Support

In the web world, it has become traditional not to offer direct technical support. But with APIs, especially if you have partners who are paying you or private customers who are an important part of your business, the situation is different. In the private API model, higher availability, both via email and possibly in person meetings, will almost certainly be part of the game. For the public API (and for some partner relationships), the question is not whether to offer support, but how much? Is web-only support, email-only support, or forms filled in on a webpage enough, or do you actually need to have a 24/7 phone number, manned by a support center, with guaranteed response times? These types of decisions will ultimately be determined based on who the target segment audiences are for the API and their expectations, contractually or otherwise.

You may want to consider having plans in place to:

- Proactively monitor assets to catch problems while they're small
- Have a system for notifying the people in charge if something goes wrong
- Have an escalation plan in place
- Track support requests to ensure that they are not forgotten or ignored
- Prioritize support requests so that the biggest issues and most important customers are given priority

Documenting Your API

Is your API easy to use? Does it have good documentation? Is it really easy to find and access on your site? Do you have tools that help developers use it?

Developers will tell you that good, clear documentation is key to their ability to program against your API. If you are serving internal developers, documentation is equally critical to attracting and maintaining usage. It is vital to support the ecosystem you are creating with your API.

Successful programs not only offer clear documentation but they also recognize that developers don't have a lot of time (or inclination) to sit down and read it. One best practice comes to us from AccuWeather's highly successful API program, which reduced its API documentation to a brief PowerPoint with the basics. "The key is to not only make the API easy to understand, but also make our documentation approachable," says Steve Smith, CIO, AccuWeather. "We realized that developers didn't have hours to sit down and read a dense document. We boiled our documentation down to a 15 slide PowerPoint that we also give in a webinar, and we localized this PowerPoint into all our key developer languages."

In general, the better the API, the easier it is for developers to figure out how to use it based on patterns that become obvious through repetition. The "Pragmatic REST" architectural style, introduced in Chapter 5, is a great way to make an API that is intuitively obvious to many developers. Intuitiveness does have limitations, however;

that's when developers need documentation. Documentation should be easy to find and use. Make it clear what to expect from the operating environment of the API:

- How to obtain the status of the API (the status page, described earlier)
- How to diagnose error codes, and what to do about them
- How to provide feedback
- How to understand monitoring

Reading documentation is a last stop rather than a first stop for many. It's advisable to have complete documentation available, but you may find that the first layer of explanation should be a querying and navigating tool that makes it easy to find relevant information quickly to start working with the API.

Apigee has the API Console for this purpose (see Figure 8-2), which uses an intuitive interface. Developers can play around with the API before committing to it, generating queries, testing results, and uncovering possible hiccups in the process. In this way, the API Console obviates the need for (and is definitely more fun than) certain kinds of documentation.

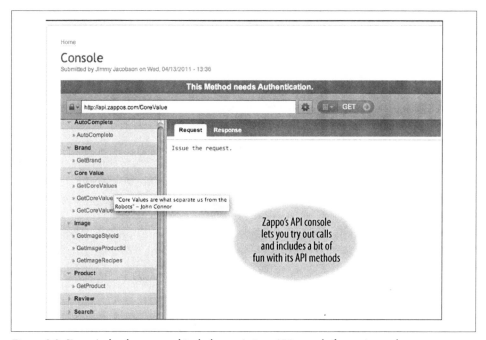

Figure 8-2. Zappo's developer portal includes an Apigee API console for testing code

Having said this, good documentation is a key success factor for an API. A strong search facility for your documentation—and excellence in keeping it up to date—help developers in getting started with your API.

Consider having two kinds of documentation:

- *Reference documentation that may be auto-generated for completeness*: It should document every API call, every parameter, and every result so that developers can be 100 percent clear on how the API functions.
- *Documentation that helps developers get started quickly*: It should be written by a professional and then carefully reviewed by experienced developers and key partners. This type of documentation explains key concepts and accelerates understanding. Without this, developers may flail through the reference documentation without being able to make connections that could appear obvious to insiders.

The documentation should include other key details, including authentication models, branding and attribution requirements, terms of use, and other information that helps the developers understand what they can and cannot do with the API.

Operations Runbook

The API team also needs documentation. Operations, in particular, needs a "runbook" that details responses to common problems. This document can help you move from an "all hands on deck" start-up to a smoothly run, professionally managed operation. Your runbook should be able to complete sentences such as:

- "If the load balancer fails..."
- "If the app server crashes..."
- "If CPU usage on the app servers is more than 75 percent..."
- "If a customer calls and says that they can't use the API..."

Traffic Management Approaches

Like any other highly available service, an API deluged with traffic can crash or deliver poor performance. How can you prevent that? Traffic floods can come from poorly coded applications or from malicious attacks. Whatever the origin of the flood, you have to safeguard the system from excessive traffic. API practitioners refer to the various ways to control API traffic as *traffic management*. Other terms such as "rate limiting" and "throttling" are also used by various people. In this section we attempt to propose some specific terms for different purposes.

There are both business and technical motives for controlling the amount of traffic that an API handles. Rather than lump them all together we'll break them into three parts:

- Quotas limit the amount of traffic to an API for business reasons. We introduced quotas in Chapter 5 and will elaborate here.
- Throttling delays the responses to certain API calls in order to put a limit on throughput.

- Spike arresting stops traffic spikes that might be caused by buggy clients or by attackers.

All APIs should have some level of spike arresting if for no other reason than to protect from disaster. Whether quotas or throttling should be deployed depends on the business requirements of the API.

Business-Level Traffic Management

There are a number of solid business reasons to control the amount of traffic that is accepted by an API. These include:

- The desire to offer tiered API access, with less access for new applications than for carefully tested and vetted applications
- The desire to sell premium access to the API, creating service tiers
- The desire to monetize the API by charging for additional traffic
- The inability to support a model in which an unlimited number of API calls can be made for free
- Discouraging or preventing abuse of the API (case in point: checking one's Twitter "timeline" hundreds or thousands of times a second in order to find out about changes more quickly than others)
- Keeping track of customer data usage (especially if the business is paying for that data)

For *public* APIs, traffic management provides a way to monetize an API. An API provider can sell "buckets" of API access or offer limited access for free and charge for higher-volume access.

For *private* APIs, however, traffic management is also useful, because it makes it possible for a business unit to offer API access to critical internal systems with a controlled amount of risk. With appropriate business-level traffic management policies in place, it is possible to offer limited API access to any developer who signs up, while ensuring that the traffic from those APIs is limited until they have asked for and been granted a larger quota.

Quotas

The traffic management feature most often used to implement business-level traffic management is a *quota*. A quota protects the API by allowing only a certain number of API calls to be made in a time period—once the quota has been reached; subsequent API calls are rejected with an error message.

Quotas are typically expressed in a number of API calls that can be accepted in an hour, a day, and occasionally a week or a month. Think of a quota like a prepaid telephone calling card—once you have it, you are entitled to a certain number of minutes and then the phone company hangs up.

Quotas are attached to an application or to an end user. There are good reasons for each approach.

It makes sense to *attach a quota to an application* as a way to control which developers have unlimited API access and which have restricted usage. Depending on the API, this can have a powerful effect on risk management. An online banking API, for instance, may wish to restrict new applications to a small amount of API traffic until they have been carefully vetted to ensure that they do not contain malicious code. That way, the risk exposure is mitigated, because the application can only do harm through a certain number of API calls. Quotas are usually attached to applications by assigning each application an API key, or through the "consumer key" issued to each application when the OAuth protocol is used. (See Chapter 6).

In other cases, it makes sense to attach a quota to a user. For example, Twitter is a prominent user of per-user quotas, since each Twitter user gets an API quota of (currently) 150 API calls per hour. This prevents clients from checking their "timelines" excessively. Without it, Twitter would be unable to function. For customers who are willing to pay and must have access to a higher volume of traffic, Twitter offers other options for a fee.

A good quota implementation requires more than counting API calls and rejecting them. For example, each application and user may need a way to request an increased quota, which requires infrastructure and some sort of management API or UI that can be used by the internal API team. In addition, customers may make a mistake and require a quota reset in order to test or deploy to the API. If so, they will contact customer care, who will require a way to see their quota and possibly reset it.

A quota, which for business reasons is a single threshold that may persist for an hour or for a week, must be relatively consistent across various servers in a cluster, or even around the world, and may need to be persisted to prevent losing the state of the quota in the event of a failure. Doing this in a totally consistent way, without any downtime due to failure, is actually not possible, as shown in the "CAP Theorem" introduced by Dr. Eric Brewer. As a result, there are really only two ways to implement a quota. First, either keep each quota count on a single server, using "failover" techniques to switch over if that server fails. Or, maintain a quota that is distributed among multiple servers, but accept the fact that, in the event of a failure, some users or applications might be granted a little "extra" in the event of a failure.

Questions to ask about quotas:

- Do you need to keep track of daily or monthly usage to measure business consumption?
- Do you need to define different consumption levels for different service tiers?

- If someone goes over the quota, what is the best business recourse? Call them up and upsell them? Or shut them off?
- If you are paying for the data, are you measuring this for billing and pricing?

Throttling

Throttling is a different technique that restricts API usage, not by rejecting API calls, but instead by slowing them down. The result puts less of a strain on critical backend resources without causing downtime for applications that use the API. Some Amazon web services, for example, are frequent but little-known users of throttling.

Throttling is friendlier for API clients because it prevents them from receiving error messages that they may not have had a chance to test for in advance. However, it is more difficult to implement, because a large number of API calls must still be accepted, and stored *somewhere*. Typically, a server in the chain of API calls, such as the API gateway, can implement throttling by tracking the incoming traffic rate and delaying API calls that have exceeded the throttling limit. However, these incoming API calls are still stored in memory and placed in a queue, awaiting processing. It is important in this case that the API gateway be configured to buffer only as many messages as memory allows and to reject API calls that might cause the API gateway to run low on memory.

If throttling makes sense for your API, then how do you determine what rate limit to throttle each client to? In this case, throttling and quotas are essentially the same—the same questions you should ask when setting an API quota apply to throttling as well.

Operational Traffic Management

Regardless of the business needs, an API operations team will need a way to ensure that the API stays up, regardless of traffic spikes caused by legitimate interest, buggy clients, or malicious attacks. Here, API traffic management is part of a chain of protections that includes firewalls, intrusion-detection systems, and IP routing and load balancing policies. It does not replace existing IT best practices for these facilities, but adds an additional and powerful layer of protection.

In turn, data derived from use of the API (API analytics) can assist with load balancing. Tim Madewell of Innotas says, "We also use API analytics to assist with load balancing —balancing resources based on end-user activity and API user activity, which we refer to as the total customer footprint."

Spike Arresting

Developers might inadvertently write some inefficient code. Someone might try to download all your data through your API. Seldom (but not never), a malicious attack is staged.

The most common mechanism for this type of traffic management is *spike arresting*, a technical backstop to prevent the system from crashing. It is a safety valve that can shut down denial-of-service (DOS) attacks or any hyperactive behavior that goes beyond a certain limit. Intrusion detection sensors and firewalls are also methods to control spikes. Regardless of the business strategy, it makes sense for just about every API to have some sort of a spike-arresting policy in place to prevent out-of-control clients from causing major problems for the API. Otherwise, the API provider must not only worry about malicious usage of the API, but also the far more likely case of clueless or incompetent consumers, who make programming mistakes that result in excessive API use as their programs spiral out of control during development (think about what happens when an endless loop occurs in an automatically scaled cloud environment; it's not a pretty sight when that traffic hits your servers).

Spike arresting is designed to function when the load is extremely high, so it must be fast and horizontally scalable. Unlike quotas, which require some sort of distributed consistency, a spike arrest must perform at it best when traffic is out of control. Spike arrestors must be implemented with an eye to maximum performance and scalability —that means no cross-cluster communications, no LAN traffic, and no disk storage.

Pitfalls to Avoid with Rate Limits and Quotas

Wrong Time Interval. Some API providers substitute quotas for rate limits—telling developers they can have a number of transactions per day. But measuring against daily quotas can leave backend systems vulnerable to short bursts of traffic. Per-second rate limits aren't a great way to create tiers of business-level consumption. You might need both quotas and rate limits.

Squishy SLAs. Some companies establish an SLA, only to say "call us if you need more." One SaaS company started this way, but found it was tough to tell important customers to manage their API usage. They eventually eased into the traffic management discussion by first providing the customer with usage reports, saying "All your requests come in on Monday at 9 AM. We love you, but can you help us?"

Assuming all requests are equal. Some requests contain many transactions or big messages, so a simple request per second-rate limit might not be sufficient.

Traffic Management and Scalability

APIs can encounter numerous operational problems, including malicious attacks and volume inundations, for which you should be prepared. Though by no means a bulletproof insurance policy, a well-designed API architecture can help mitigate many of these potential issues.

Most APIs are somewhat analogous to websites and to other modern, scalable applications in terms of their network architecture. At first, websites were just made of a single web server, connected to the Internet. Soon after public Internet use became available, operators added firewalls to prevent data from entering through the wrong port. Typically, intrusion detection systems were installed at the firewall level to flag (or halt) unusual traffic patterns.

Once multiple servers became part of the picture, a load balancer was needed to distribute traffic to the different servers and ensure high availability. Dedicated web servers for static content, application servers, databases, and data caches completed the scene. As more websites became distributed, DNS became more than a way to map a URI to an IP address—it became a mechanism for distributing traffic around the world based on the location of the client, and for failing over during a disaster from one data center to another. As high volume became a consideration, CDNs, consisting of ranks of machines that cached popular web pages in multiple geographic locations, grew popular as way of reducing access latency. Now, many website operators place this workload in the cloud with services such as Amazon EC2, in order to avoid running a data center entirely. Indeed, many private and public applications now run completely "in the cloud" this way.

An Evolving Approach to Caching at the New York Times

We spoke with Derek Willis, Newsroom Developer at the NYT, and asked him about concerns about scaling.

"We have had to pay a lot of attention to maintaining our APIs and now we have a dedicated team that handles that. We've been moving to a cloud infrastructure over time (through Mashery).

We've also learned a lot about caching. We've had to make a lot of changes to our caching approach as customer activity has grown. We've gone from ordinary page caching to memcached and now we use Varnish for fine-grained response caching.

The point is—like many things, caching keeps evolving. At times we underestimate and have to go back and understand how to scale and support it. But we keep evolving our strategy as traffic increases."

API Gateways

Just as firewalls, intrusion detection sensors, and load balancers solved particular problems for web applications, over time specific pieces of infrastructure have evolved around web services and specifically around APIs.

An API gateway performs tasks such as caching, security, logging, auditing, and transformation, acting as a layer of abstraction between the application server layer that runs the API and the device that accesses the API. The gateway layer handles common infrastructure tasks, freeing up the application server to perform the calculations and transformations needed to deliver content and process requests. By having a layer that offloads tasks from complicated, expensive backend application servers and abstracts them away from what the developer sees, the API can have a simpler, more flexible architecture.

Sectioning off the gateway helps each tier of the architecture specialize in discrete areas. The gateway deals with traffic management, such as authentication, security, and routing. The API servers deal with request and response handling. A third tier, the data source tier, can be inserted to normalize data management—such as recognizing that "J. Public," "Joe Public," and "Joseph Public" are all the same person.

An API gateway can reduce the workload on the backend application servers that support the API by reducing the number of tasks that they must handle. For example, by offloading rate limiting and even some data transformation from the application servers, they can run with less memory, use less CPU, or, if they are based on commercial products, even require fewer software licenses to run. An API gateway can also protect the backend from API-specific security risks such as SQL injection and XML attacks.

Keep in mind that not all web server technologies handle high throughput well, and some do not handle a large number of concurrent connections. Because it can act as a proxy between the API clients and the backend, an API gateway can offload connection management, turning a large number of connections between the devices that invoke the API into a smaller number of connections to the backend. This, again, can reduce latency as well as the need for backend server resources.

Finally, the API gateway not only reduces load on the backend server itself; it also reduces the load on the development team—and in most companies, developers are more expensive than servers or software licenses. By avoiding the need to build features such as OAuth security, rate limiting, and caching from scratch, or by assembling a list of third-party components, the development team can spend more time delivering the API's functionality.

Solutions to many of the issues described elsewhere in this chapter can be offloaded to an API gateway if desired, whether the API gateway is a commercial product, built from open source, built from scratch, or some combination. These issues include:

- Supporting security schemes such as OAuth, HTTP Basic authentication, SAML, and SSL
- Implementing traffic management policies to limit the amount of API calls that are accepted
- Caching frequent API results to reduce response times and reduce load on the backend
- Transforming API requests and responses from one format into another—for example, to turn an existing SOAP-based web service into a REST API that supports both XML and JSON without requiring a new version of the server

- Data transformations and URI-rewriting rules that can sometimes make it possible to support an older version of an API without necessarily maintaining two versions of the backend servers

Approaches to API Gateways in the Cloud

As more API services are sourced and distributed in the cloud, the concept of CDNs can also apply to APIs. API gateways can be placed in the cloud and act as an intermediate proxy layer, caching some traffic before it ever gets to your network. API gateways can also be deployed in various geographical locations, behind dynamic DNS services that route API clients to the nearest gateway. Only traffic that is legitimate and which was not previously cached needs to be forwarded to the "origin" API backend servers, which may be restricted to only one or two data centers.

Also, because common languages used for APIs are based on HTTP, traditional CDN providers such as Akamai can be used for certain kinds of API traffic. One simple way to do this is to return a URI that points to a CDN location—this is how Netflix serves up huge video files, for instance. For some types of APIs and content, the API can even return an HTTP error code to redirect the client to a traditional CDN in order to retrieve a result directly. (However, clients must be correctly configured to follow HTTP redirects, so this technique should be used with care.)

CHAPTER 9

Measuring the Success of Your API

Hopefully, a lot of traffic and business will come through the API. As a result, you'll need metrics for a variety of reasons, including operational reasons as well as for measuring the success of the API and gauging how it is being used.

Let's face it: It's hard to improve what you don't measure, so we suggest baking your business model into the API. For example, if your company sells ads, you need to know how the API affects your ad-supported business. If your company sells cars, you need to know the API supports your company's ability to sell cars effectively.

Different types of APIs need to measure different things. Some of what we discuss in this chapter may not apply to your API (for example, content-focused APIs need different metrics than transactional APIs). To add an extra twist, what you measure will change over time. The point is to establish some metrics as a starting point, then see what others you need.

The bottom line is that analytics provide you with information to make future decisions. That information might mean a variety of different things. It might indicate that traffic is up because the API is succeeding, but a surge of traffic could mean that the API is being used inefficiently, resulting in inflated traffic.

The more you know, the better you'll be able to see and demonstrate what is going on. You'll need metrics to help you decide which features to add and how to evolve the API. And sometimes you'll have a hunch that something is happening (the surge in traffic indicates that API traffic is increasing) and then have to develop metrics to help demonstrate what you already know to the rest of the team.

Handling API Metrics

Here are some things that we have found helpful when setting up API analytics:

Get early buy-in on the top 3
> Focus on one to three top-level strategic metrics and get early, wide agreement from all parts of the team: the sponsoring executive, project manager, engineering

head, business development, and operations manager. If different stakeholders measure success using different metrics (say, number of developer sign-ups vs. API traffic vs. revenue), this can pull resources in different directions.

Track against realistic projections

Set expectations early by modeling anticipated results, and then track actuals against this estimate. For a private API, you might project that mobile product teams can innovate on their products 50 percent faster than prior to the API. For a public API, you might make projections on the community engagement, such as 20 percent of registered developers might build an app, 10 percent of those apps might drive ongoing traffic, each of those apps might drive a certain volume of traffic, and so on.

Publish a weekly dashboard

Proactively highlight product updates and community activities that do or don't change your key metrics so that you can quickly adjust tactics and think of new ideas to improve the metrics.

Why Capture Usage Metrics?

Usage metrics help providers understand how business customers are interacting with your products, services, or content through apps that are served by the API. This has less to do with the specific business assets that are valuable to your customers than it does with the way they are interacting with the features available to them. For example, a media company like The Guardian offers a variety of apps through which readers can get content. These apps are consuming The Guardian APIs and delivering content to these users. The Guardian could potentially track usage patterns on readers consuming stories on different apps, including which stories or topics are more popular on which devices, what times of day or days of the week they are most active per device, and so on. Because all of these apps are served by the same API, it makes sense for the API to capture usage patterns and provide metrics around them.

The high-level usage metrics to consider capturing include:

- What was requested and by whom?
- What did the API deliver for a given request?
- What did the device actually show the user?
- What did the user do with what was shown?

Armed with such data, content decisions can be made on a more granular level. For example: "What sports stories did end users read on the iPhone between noon and 4 PM on weekends?" Answer that, and you can trace what each user was presented and how it translated into an interaction on that device. Perhaps a certain type of story performs better on Android apps. Maybe these usage patterns suggest that stories on politics perform better than sports on weekend afternoons, so you may decide to re-order the topic lists between noon and 4 PM on weekends.

Innotas tracks trends in usage. "We use API trend reporting at a macro level over time —common calls, common integration. This gets fed into product management, sales, and performance tuning to make the product better," says Tim Madewell.

Requests and Responses

Although the number of requests is a useful metric, it only tells part of the story. Requests do not translate into end-user consumption—they merely create opportunities for consumption. To put it another way, tracking requests reveals information about how apps access the API even though the API itself is really just a means of getting content in front of end users. So it is critical for producers of content APIs to track how the content is consumed when distributed through the API.

In an API, every request has a response, which also tells part of the story. Although request metrics tell us what the developer asked for, they do not tell us what was delivered. Depending on the nature of the API, the response may include multiple items for each request, warning or error codes, or other information returned to the user. Obviously, when you're analyzing responses, errors are handled in a different way from successful responses, which indicate everything is working fine.

Requests and response metrics are useful in understanding a lot about how the API works, what trends are emerging in what is being asked for, and what is being delivered in response. But what these metrics don't convey is how this is translating into value for your end user. To understand what end users are doing with the business assets, you will need to map request and response metrics to data that you capture from the client apps themselves.

Impressions

Impressions are the first point in the metrics calculation that captures actual consumption. An *impression* is a page view or equivalent, where an end user experiences the content that was delivered by the API.

This is a very important metric because impressions measure the number of "eyeballs" that see the content delivered by the API. For example, some requests are never presented to a user if the calling application never presents them. Additionally, some calling applications may cache content and present it multiple times from one request. Moreover, because a single request could return multiple items in a response, depending on how the requesting application handles it, there could be many impressions for that single request. As a result, the impression numbers could be substantially higher or lower than the request and/or response totals. This metric could have greater relevance for some business models, such as those driven by ad revenue, because ad revenue is driven by what is displayed not what is requested.

There are a couple of methods for capturing this metric. One common way is by placing an image beacon in a piece of the content. The beacon signals from the API's server when it is presented by the calling application, providing the API publisher with information about content consumption every time it is viewed. This is particularly effective for APIs with a large number of calling applications, some of which may be unknown to the API provider (including public API developers). The drawback, however, is that it typically requires that the delivered content maintain embedded markup and that the calling applications interpret that markup effectively. Moreover, because this approach is based on image rendering, it is possible that the impression actually happens without any eyeballs seeing it (if the content gets rendered in a hidden div, for example).

For more sophisticated systems, particularly when the calling applications are managed by the API provider, another approach is to add a callback function that returns information to the API from the calling application, detailing what the application actually showed the users. This is much more powerful and accurate but is harder to maintain over time and with a growing number of developers.

Loyalty

Once an API receives an impression, the next step is to create some relationships around how end users interact with the content. After the user consumed a piece of content, did he or she move on to another piece of content? Or do they have trackable sessions in the system already, perhaps from a different platform (whether delivered from the API or not)? There are several ways to try to track these relationships, but it is quite challenging. The challenge is to ensure that all users can be tracked based on their usage, regardless of platform. This will be especially difficult for services that do not require a login or if there is a high rate of users who terminate their login or their cookies. To the extent that these threads in usage can be tracked, it will help provide clarity on how the applications are used and what their value is for your customers. Important trends in usage can be established with only a subset of data, so it is more important to set it up to capture the data in some cases than to make sure that you account for cookie-killers and other scenarios that can snap the trend lines.

Operational Metrics

This section covers some guidelines for designing operational metrics.

The most successful web analytics tools, such as Google Analytics, work by running JavaScript inside the browser for each page to be tracked. This allows the analytics system to gather data about many aspects of the page and system, which helps offer deeper insight into the users' behavior. They also can employ tracking mechanisms such as one-pixel "beacon" graphics to determine when a user views a certain page.

This technique doesn't work for APIs. To start with, unlike a web page there's no way for an API response to force the client to do anything. And although APIs are consumed by web applications running inside browsers, often they are also consumed by mobile devices, servers, and inside other environments where running JavaScript isn't even possible.

(In a private API, on the other hand, the API provider sometimes has complete control over what happens in the client. In those cases, using techniques like JavaScript and beacon graphics to track usage is indeed possible.)

Instead, API analytics have to be generated on the server side – either inside the server that serves up the API traffic directly, or from a layer that sits in front of those servers. That means that certain pieces of information, such as the exact software version of the client, are not available unless the client sends a correct value in an HTTP header.

However, there is a rich set of data to mine inside API traffic. Since API traffic is typically self-describing (it is possible to extract pieces of data from XML and JSON without having access to special code on the client or server side), it is possible to insert tools at any layer that can determine not only what traffic is hitting the API, but also what it means to the business. For instance, information such as the amount of money spent on a product, the number of items ordered, and the amount of media content returned to a client can all be extracted without changing the client *or the server*.

This gives API-based analytics an advantage over the system-level logs available from most application servers. Rather than a file that lists IP addresses, URIs, and error codes, the API provider can build a rich database of business-level information.

This data can have multiple uses. "Our customers write code that creates calls that read and write tens of thousands of records," said Tim Madewell of Innotas. "Absolutely our first requirement was visibility; you can't govern what you can't see. The problem was that all of this activity was intermingled in the system logs with all the other system-generated events. We needed visibility to be able to relate calls and reconstruct what happened with meaningful data."

This information was important not only to Innotas internally, but also improved their ability to support API customers. "Before, when a customer called and said 'it's not working right,' all we could say was 'go look at your code.' But with API analytics we can capture the payload—trap the data for the customer—and use our API debugging tools to help them ID the problem message," said Madewell.

Categories of metrics that most businesses will care about include effectiveness, performance, and usage metrics.

Effectiveness Metrics

Effectiveness metrics help the company understand how to make the API more effective at satisfying existing business strategies. For example, Netflix noticed that it was receiving upwards of 30 billion requests per month and that some of the interfaces supporting the API were exceedingly "chatty." In other words, clients needed to make a lot more API calls to get the job done than was necessary, which slows down each client and results in more load on backend systems. This chattiness is an indication that the API is not serving its clients as effectively as it could. That understanding is helping to drive major design changes for the next version of the API. As a result, those design changes should result in improvements in overall performance for apps that use the API, which in turn could translate into improved customer satisfaction. Meanwhile, these changes will also lower overall costs for API system maintenance and will improve the efficiency of the internal app developers, allowing new features and/or apps to hit the market faster. Effectiveness metrics can often be analyzed over longer periods of time.

Performance Metrics

Metrics that track overall API performance include error rates, types of errors, system performance, latencies in request handling, and timeouts. Such metrics should be monitored over time. Additions to the API should not slow it down. These kinds of metrics often tie in directly to the SLAs and monitoring systems that are in place for real-time responses when thresholds are met. Particular attention should be paid to the impact of code and system changes, by monitoring the effects on internal servers as well as the experience on the developer side.

Capturing Metrics at Innotas

Innotas is a leading provider of cloud solutions for IT management. We spoke with Tim Madewell, Senior Vice President of Professional Services.

"We designed metrics to answer the following key questions about the API:

- What customers are calling the APIs?
- What APIs are they calling? How frequently?

Our first dashboard had only these two levels as we sought understanding, but then we added:

- How many customers are hitting me, and how frequently are they hitting me?
- How many customers are using a particular service?
- What operations in an API are they hitting?

Next we added deeper analytics to answer what they were doing with the API. We broke this down into two parts:

Functional attributes
  Can we drill down to understand what they are doing a bit more?

Unusual behavior
  For example, we had customers who were accidentally updating all of their reference data every 10 minutes."

Key Questions to Ask about API Performance

Here is a list of critical questions to ask in support of developing appropriate metrics for your API:

- Who are the key audiences for the API?
- How will the key audiences use the API?
- How does this usage map to existing business models and KPIs?
- What are their usage patterns? How do the usage patterns for certain consumers relate to other consumers of the API?
- How "good" is your service?
- What latency do customers experience, by request and by region?
- How many errors and user-experienced bugs are happening and how often?
- What kind of service is the API delivering compared with any formal Service Level Agreement agreed to or paid for?
- What do you mean by "down time" and how much is your API experiencing?
- How can you find out if a customer is having a problem (before they call)?
- How is the API usage impacting the rest of the platform or web products that use the same API?
- Can you quickly trap and debug based on a specific message? Based on what is in a cache?
- Who are the top priority customers? Internal staff? Partners? The public developer community?
- Who should you call to upsell to a higher-service tier or to formulate a new deal?
- What do you need to show general management to make product strategy (or tactical) decisions?
- Will you need to create audit trails or metering reports for partners that are paying for API access?
- Do you need to create metrics based on a certain data value in the payload (such as a specific product SKU)?
- What is the cost of the data that you are serving (if you are licensing this data)?

These questions become increasingly important when opening a service as an API—delivery times are critical when customers, contract terms, and compliance regulations come into play.

How Metrics Evolved at NPR

NPR used metrics to evaluate and improve its API's impact on the business and their ability to better serve their end-user audience. A look back at the history of the NPR

API is instructive. Use of the NPR API grew tremendously since its 2008 launch. Figure 9-1 shows growth in requests to the NPR API over time.

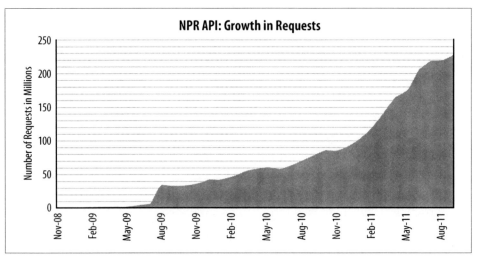

Figure 9-1. Requests to the NPR API

A big jump in *API requests* from July to August 2010 followed the launch of many new products in July. Among them were a relaunch of NPR.org, the NPR.org Flash Player, and the NPR News iPhone app, WBUR's new website, and Minnesota Public Radio's new site. Since then, an increasing number of applications were implemented on the API, including the NPR mobile site and other station sites (like KQED and KPCC), accounting for the steady growth near the right side of the chart. Although requests are only one part of the picture, it is still a good proxy for demonstrating overall growth for NPR's distribution and app strategy.

In October 2009, NPR started tracking the total number of stories delivered by the API to the calling application (Figure 9-2). Note that stories requested is not necessarily the number presented to or consumed by end users.

Although NPR received more than 72 million requests to the API in August 2010, it delivered more than 1.3 billion stories in that timeframe. This translates into roughly 18 stories per request. Clearly, capturing only request data left out a very important part of the story.

Content that contains an audio or video asset provides a tangible example of an impression. Generating an impression of a story is the first step. If the user then clicks on the audio, that click-through should also be attributed to the session attached to the API impression by passing tracking information to the audio URI so that the audio can be related to the page view. By creating opportunities for the API content to create serendipitous experiences with other content, the content API becomes stronger.

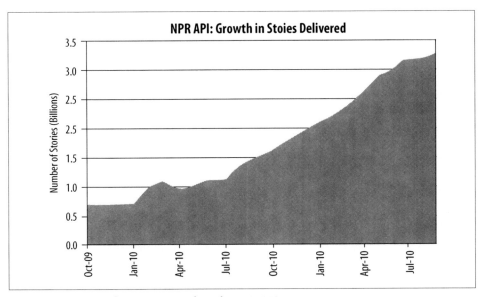

Figure 9-2. Number of stories requested via the NPR API

Capturing data for each of these metrics offers unique challenges. For example, to improve performance of its APIs, NPR uses a suite of caching layers. Moreover, the API has many rights-exclusion algorithms and transformations. As a result, it is increasingly difficult to ensure successful tracking of all of the metrics for all of the requests. Tracking impressions from APIs offers unique challenges, since much of the content is distributed in XML, JSON, or something comparable. How can a tracking beacon be placed in the content? In which field should it go, and how can the API owner be sure that the calling application will consume that field? If it's placed in multiple fields to ensure consumption, how do you prevent duplicate hits for a single page view? Alternatively, if you have control over the calling apps, you may be able to have the app capture the impression metrics and send them back to the server. Putting that responsibility on the application, however, requires some degree of consistency across the calling applications, which can be tough to orchestrate.

NPR had some ideas as to how to gauge success of its private API from a metrics perspective, including overall traffic to and from the API and growth of the API relative to tangible business metrics like page views or ad impressions. For the public API, other metrics were established, including number of registered developers, adoption by member stations, and total number of requests. That said, having one of the first comprehensive content APIs for a media company, it was hard to determine what the numbers meant. In a few weeks, NPR had more than 300 registrants. Was that good? It was hard to know. Late in 2008, the NPR API had two million requests per month. That seemed really good, but after the internal adoption in July of 2009, when the traffic spiked to almost 40 million requests per month, the original numbers no longer seemed impressive.

Despite the challenges in figuring out what the numbers meant, NPR believed that the numbers were a strong indication of success for the API and worthy of further investment.

Over time, NPR has become the biggest consumer of its own API by a large margin. This shift, which we have seen many times, also caused NPR to shift its metrics. The metrics NPR started with are not the ones they currently use to gauge how the API is doing today.

CHAPTER 10

Engaging Developers to Drive Adoption

You've built a great API and have the operational bases covered, but having an API doesn't matter if nobody is using it. Evangelizing and marketing your API is critical to adoption, no matter what type of API you have. Even if the API is private, such as an API for your internal employees or a SaaS API intended only for your partners, it still needs to be promoted.

Let's face it: no matter what type of API you offer, developers make or break your API strategy. They are your greatest source of feedback, your best advocates, and your toughest critics. If you keep your eye on making developers successful, you are building on a strong foundation.

The following sections describe how to think about driving adoption for your target audiences. Although we will spend time on each, in this chapter, we admit that public APIs get more attention. Engaging developers is every bit as important with private APIs, but the approaches tend to be more targeted to the developer community. Internal developers might be more demanding and tell you straight up what they need; they may also have some resistance to new ways of doing things (APIs, REST, JSON) that you won't find with developers being targeted by public APIs. The approach for partner developers with a private API really depends on your partner community, so you'll have to be the judge of what engagement strategies are going to work best. A big (or widening) partner community for a private API is really more like a public API in that you want to increase the number of developers and their level of engagement. The point is that no matter who you are trying to engage, you need to think hard about who they are, what they need, what earns their respect, and what motivates them to work with your API.

What Motivates Developers?

Developers are smart, busy, and have lots of options. To reach developers, it pays to understand what motivates them to choose one platform, productivity tool, or API over another.

We have observed that the most successful developer programs focus on solving one or more of these developer problems: saving developers time, building their skills and resume, or getting them paid!

This can work much more effectively than traditional marketing efforts or promotions that focus on your API and your brand. In fact, you'll often hear developers talking about how much they *hate* traditional marketing with its vendor-centric approach and by anything that takes their support for granted.

Key Parts of a Developer Program Offering

By observing the best developer programs, you can see many approach the practice of driving adoption on several levels, which include:

Product
> Your API and why developers should use it

Access
> Making it fast and easy to be successful using the API in a self-service fashion

Business terms
> Setting expectations with developers on usage terms and benefits

Content
> Supporting materials that get developers started and inspire great ideas

Awareness
> Evangelizing your API to the target audience

Experience
> The end-to-end customer experience of learning and using the API

Community
> Resources for support and collaboration

Product (or First You Need a Great API!)

First and foremost, you must have a solid API. Developers have many options, and having a cool API is critical to convincing them to move from their status quo. If your API is popular enough, you can get away with having a less than perfect developer program or assets.

As we discussed earlier, it's really important to communicate how your API is different from others that might be similar or seem just like it. Whether it's having richer data, more features, better terms, or some other distinction—remember that you may be trying to convince someone to stop using an existing approach and try your API.

Access to Your API and to You

Once you have a strong API, you need to make it easy and fast to try with successful results. Developers should be able to get up and running quickly, ideally being able to register and become productive in less than five minutes. Even if your API requires establishing a formal partner relationship, you can still provide at least one operation that does not require registration to whet their appetite. One example is Twitter, which offers its timeline API operation without requiring authentication.

Derek Gottfrid says of his work at the *New York Times*, "The more we lowered the bar for developers to get involved, the better response we got. For example, we offered code samples and mashup examples highlighting the best use cases of the API." Developer outreach was equally important at the *Times*. "We also took the time to get traction with the developer community. There's no magic there, just a lot of hard work—a lot of staying on top of it," said Gottfrid. "We had one community manager that worked with developers using about a dozen APIs. We had one developer per API and a product manager that helped with productization."

Access also means access to you! Your team should be highly available and responsive to developer inquiries. "In general, it's just really important to be responsive," suggests Derek Willis of the *New York Times*. "If we don't have an answer for a forum question right away, we'll still answer it right away so that the developer knows that there is someone working on it. If developers think they are just talking to a wall, they will go away."

Again, all these points are not just for the public API programs—they also apply to private APIs. Some of the toughest developers to win over can be your colleagues!

Business Terms and SLA Expectations

The best developer programs are clear and proactive in setting developer expectations about whether they will need to pay for services, expectations around SLAs (or not), and restrictions, if any.

Often APIs are launched without having every detail about terms and business model figured out. If you're not sure how you will eventually monetize the program, put any caveats about future expected use in the terms. For example, most of the consumer maps API programs made it clear that terms could change and that heavy users would be asked to pay.

Content

As we discussed earlier, developers expect clear and accurate documentation for your API. Decent documentation might even be viewed as a competitive differentiator for your API.

But in addition to standard documentation, other types of content can greatly assist developers and speed their adoption of your API. For example, you can augment and simplify your API documentation with videos or a slideshare. Says Steve Smith of AccuWeather, "Keep your collateral simple. Realize that nobody is going to read a 50-page document."

In addition to API documentation, having a developer gallery with examples of applications and actual code that can be cut and pasted from your sample gallery into a developer app is one of the most requested developer materials, year after year. Again, the key is to get the developer up and running more quickly.

Having all of your content easily accessible from a single place, often called a developer portal, is an important part of your developer program. We'll go into more details later in this chapter.

Awareness of Your API

If you have a great API, offer easy access, set expectations for how developers will pay or get paid, then focus on getting the word out to as many developers as you can.

One of the most effective things you can do to drive awareness of your API is to get your content where developers hang out—or take the content to the developers. (Don't wait for the developers to come to you.) Sites like ProgrammableWeb.com and other developer sites and communities often have listings, app galleries, or other appropriate forums where you can post the news about your API. As long as you keep it relevant to the audience (such as good code examples and tips or tricks for building apps with your API), this can create some of the most lasting results, especially if some of these sites are always highly ranked in Google and other web search results.

You can also do traditional public relations campaign or "press" when you launch your API or at major milestones. While developers typically don't read press releases, they do follow influential tech blogs and publications, and having your PR department reach out to the outlets that cover APIs can get you some initial exposure to developers who will try your API.

Focus on the Full Developer Experience

The best developer programs put a lot of energy into ensuring that the end-to-end process from the developer's perspective is as smooth as possible across the full API lifecycle, including registration, learning, building, debugging, and deploying an app. Some ways to create a great developer experience include:

- Fast self-service signup for API access
- Productivity tools to speed development, such as test harnesses, API consoles, and sandboxes (test environments for APIs that might work with account data)
- Engagement tools with your team and fellow developers, through forums, blogs, or developer galleries
- Easy access to support and important information such as FAQs and terms and conditions

In other words, the processes that surround your API are just as much a part of the product as your API itself.

Community

The very best developer programs foster a sense of community where developers help and inspire each other to create apps. Building a vibrant, healthy community that functions in this way is important for many reasons, but perhaps most importantly, this is often the only way to create leverage in empowering and managing a large group of possibly thousands of developers, especially if there are only 1 or 2 API community managers!

Creating community is a larger topic beyond the scope of this book, although there are some excellent resources such as *The Art of Community* by Jono Bacon. However, a key success factor is that you actively engage with influential developers in your target audience. This means both online forums (such as Twitter and StackOverflow) and also offline events such as conferences.

As Derek Willis of the *New York Times* API program puts it, "You have to do the hard stuff. You have to get out there and have actual contact with developers. That's why we try to do things like hackathons, or find other ways to bring people in for face-to-face feedback. It's important that developers know that there are real people on the other side of the API request. There is just no substitute for this."

Again, the idea is to empower developers to advocate for you and support other developers on your behalf.

The Anatomy of a Developer Portal

API programs typically have a developer portal that serves as the resource center for the API. It offers a site for API registration, a learning resource, an engagement site, and a reflection of your community.

Developer portals share some common elements, but they differ in their approach to those elements.

The *New York Times* developer network (Figure 10-1) looks almost like a newspaper page. It offers links to all the information new developers need, from getting started info to an API console to branding information and even a rationale for using the API ("Why just read the news when you can hack it?")

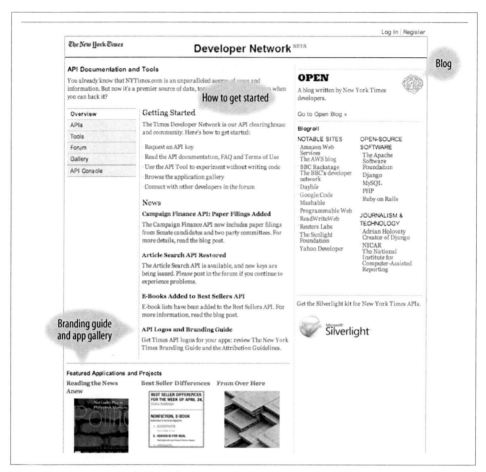

Figure 10-1. The New York Times developer network

eBay's page (Figure 10-2) focuses on news about the API. Content for new developers is not as prominent, but note the business benefits stated concisely in the upper right corner.

eBay's API has been around so long that its portal seems to target existing developers, but clearly outlines the business benefits of the API.

Facebook's API (Figure 10-3) offers many opportunities for developer engagement, from video how-to information to portals targeted at specific kinds of developers.

Figure 10-2. The eBay API developer portal

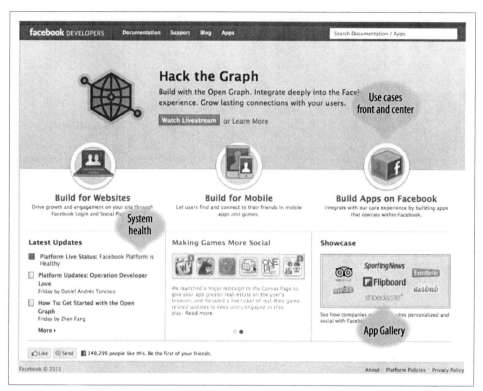

Figure 10-3. Facebook's developer portal

The design of the Twitter developer portal is minimalistic, consistent with Twitter itself. It overtly targets new developers. Developer outreach is written all over Twitter's portal, with links to terms of use as well as important news.

What this quick survey shows is that developer portals, though unique to their audience, have many of the same elements, which include:

Information about the offering
> What is the API designed to do? What are the terms for using it? What business assets does it expose? What is the process for getting started with the API? What are the benefits?

Documentation
> Getting started on the Twitter API page leads you straight to documentation where you can learn more, clearly laid out for exploration and headlined to attract developers.

An easy way to try the API
> Public APIs make registration fast so that you can try out API calls using your browser. Some, like Netflix and Twitter, ask you to quickly register an application

before you can try the API. Zappo's developer portal has an Apigee API console that enables you to try out commands.

App gallery

Developers looking for ideas can look at the app gallery on most developer portals. For instance Foursquare's (*https://foursquare.com/apps/*) gallery has a wide range of sample applications. More than just a museum of cool stuff, galleries help developers (and business owners) get ideas for how the API can be used in interesting ways.

Means of contact

There should be an easy way for the developer to get in contact with the API team. This is often handled via forums.

Ways to meet other developers in person

All this online and virtual stuff is supported by face-to-face meetings. In addition to conferences, there are less formal meetings where developers can get ideas and brainstorm with the API team. Twitter has been having "teatime" with interested developers in major cities.

Information about the business arrangement

Naturally, developers want and need to know the details of the business arrangement and the rules for using branding. With private APIs, it could be a formal partner agreement with a series of steps and legal documents. With public APIs, it can be as simple as agreeing to the terms of use. Twitter features its terms of use, called the "Developer Rules of the Road," on its developer portal and also when you apply for an account.

The Dos and Don'ts of Developer Engagement

Here are a few best practices for keeping developers engaged.

Dos

Generally speaking, simplicity, straightforwardness, openness, and authenticity win the day. Developers don't like the idea of being sold a bill of goods. Instead, they want something straightforward, which they can use to get their hands dirty right away.

Look Alive!

In the developer world, there is an expectation of fresh content on your site every two or three days. Developers also expect that your documentation is up-to-date, clear, and easy to understand.

Your website should also be vibrant and alive. This is one of the only areas of API development where a visual designer plays a key role. The content engine, sample applications, and FAQs help achieve this goal. It's an online application of the old adage, "Nothing attracts a crowd like a crowd."

Your community manager should be an active blogger who engages with the audience in a meaningful, iterative, and frequent way. The community manager should also keep the communication alive through speaking events, conferences, webinars, and just plain old meeting developers in person.

Any changes to the API, especially big changes, should be displayed prominently. Figure 10-4 shows an announcement from Twitter.

Figure 10-4. Twitter announces a big change at the top of its developer portal

Target Alpha Geeks

Once these communities have been identified, it falls to the API provider to identify the alpha geeks—a term used by Tim O'Reilly to refer to top developers who have the respect and admiration of their peers, as well as the ability to rally other developers.

Spend some time on the relevant blogs and community boards, and it won't be long before you figure out who the alpha geeks are. They post the most, respond the most, and organize activities in real life, which, contrary to popular belief, are essential to developer communities' continuity. Reach out to them—preferably in person. Get to know them, get their advice and suggestions, and consider those suggestions seriously.

The best strategy is not promoting your API as a finished product. Let developers influence your product and be part of your team. Major software companies have successfully deployed this strategy, hosting events for their top-alpha-dog public developers, working collaboratively with them, and even issuing them business cards. The point: make them part of your team, and they will help make your product better and go to bat for you.

This is not a superficial act. Alpha geeks engage in dialogue with the API provider, and actually help improve the product with their programming contributions. They then evangelize its value on blogs, Twitter feeds, and websites to other developers.

In so doing, companies are rewarded for their attentiveness and receive it in return from developers who, in many cases, wind up behaving as if they work for these companies, with a greater degree of loyalty than employees whom the company actually pays, because their individual brand profiles can be maintained.

Create Scale and Leverage

The goal of building a community of developers is to achieve scale and leverage once you have curried favor with the initial set of target communities (and their respective alpha geeks).

Once you have 20 to 40 developers in your community, you can conduct a quick internal survey to identify gaps—are you reaching all of your target segments? Are there major platforms on which you have no presence? Now is the time to begin soliciting alpha geeks for their knowledge of top developers in other niches.

Be sure to read posted conversations carefully. Initiate interactions between people who are looking for help and those who can offer help. The ultimate goal is to have those conversations happen on their own—a watershed indication that you have built a successful community.

Running contests is another way to keep participation up and bring new people into the circle. But the greatest measure of success is the degree to which the community itself begins to take over the kinds of activities you once had to feed and water.

Ultimately, the community you build will begin to grow itself because it is a self-sustaining, useful forum for exchanges of value.

Foster Developer Community

One of the best ways to make developers successful is to put them in touch with each other so that they can share information, tips, and tricks, and offer a fresh look at working with your API. Once you have made developers successful, they can start helping each other too. To engage with developers, offer tools that help them work together and discuss and share knowledge about your APIs. Blogs, documentation, forums, app galleries, and in person meetups are all important.

Kin Lane thinks blogs are the most important resource you can offer for public API communities. "Blogging is the most important piece of content I offer. Not just my blog, but on other sites like ProgrammableWeb." Effective content has to be available where developers can get to it themselves. "It's important that all content be *self-service content*. Whitepapers, FAQs, anything I can write and a developer can consume on their own," says Lane. "Even if the audience doesn't care about my API in particular for their work, it's important that I express a point of view on API technology and my experience of what's happening in the market."

Seek Out Key Influencers

For public or private APIs, there are key apps or developers that will help drive adoption through the rest of the company or community. If a significant app can be created by a team using your API, it will be substantially easier to engage others in leveraging your API for their apps. The first win is the hardest, but also the most important.

If you are launching a public API, there are superstars in the developer world that other developers follow and from whom they seek advice. These alpha developers can be a great resource for feedback. If you build a relationship with these influencers, they might carry the word about your API to their contacts or become a support advocate. Not sure how to identify these folks? Look for the developers who run meet-ups or who speak at conferences in your target segment.

Plug into Other Developer Communities

Many public API programs focus heavily on building their own "developer community" and invest all their energy into building developer portals and forum content.

While this is a great practice, don't overlook the value of plugging your content into outside developer communities. These can include large existing developer communities for the target language (such as Ruby), the platform (such as Apple's iOS) or the type of app that the target developer segment is building (such as the Amazon developer community).

Other developer communities often need great relevant content—such as guidance on how your API might complement their offering. The most effective types of content, such as example apps and how-to guides, are usually free to contribute. Developers also "hang out," read, and contribute to online communities such as Programmable-Web, StackOverflow, and many others; they read news and blogs on sites like Read-WriteWeb, Hacker News, and TechCrunch.

Don'ts

When setting out to create APIs and attract developers, here are some mistakes that companies make.

No differentiation for the API (it's just like so-and-so's API)

Oftentimes developers have multiple options and you need to provide some reason for developers to use your API. It could be more data, better terms, better service, or some other factor. The important thing is that you need to stand out.

Making it hard to sign up

Developers want to be up and productive in 5 minutes or less, providing immediate gratification. Even if your API requires formal partnership or authentication, it's a good practice to offer at least one free API method that developers can immediately use. For example, the Twitter public timeline method requires no authentication at all.

Marketing the API

Developers hate vendor pitches. Newsletters talking about your brand are likely to go unread. They want information that helps them solve problems, make money, or code faster.

Overfocus on the developer portal

Although the developer portal is a key component of an API strategy, don't underestimate the value of getting your content on other sites where developers hang out. Don't consider the portal a substitute for interaction with developers, both online and in person.

Selecting the wrong community manager

Problems include not having a full time community manager or having someone who is not technical or is an odd fit. Your community manager should be both technical and a bit extroverted and be present in both online and offline forums.

Having an overly broad focus

Instead of focusing on "everybody" or "all app types," target a smaller community. It's easier to find the influencers and get feedback. It's hard to make everybody happy, so if you target a certain niche of developers, your job will be more manageable.

CHAPTER 11

Epilogue: Just the Beginning

Steven Covey, in his widely read book *The Seven Habits of Highly Effective People*, recommends to begin with the end in mind. With a topic like APIs, a technology that can be transformative in so many ways to businesses of all sizes, keeping the end in mind can be a huge challenge. There might be one end to keep in mind, or a dozen.

Like many other technical endeavors, an API is not a one-size-fits-all solution. It is imperative for you to understand your business goals, the key audiences for the API, and your key metrics before you start. Our sincere hope is now that you have made it through this book it will be significantly easier to imagine what APIs can do to help your business.

The API world is still in its infancy. The pioneering tech companies in Silicon Valley have paved the way, showing us what works and what doesn't. Standing on the shoulders of those giants, we have a chance to see a new future for our businesses, with opportunities to expand them in ways not previously available to us. It is vital to remember that the API economies you create will work in many different ways. What Google or Amazon does in public will be different from what your organization may do in private. APIs will expose business assets in both cases and make them available through applications, but how that will happen will be quite different. We hope that you now are able to understand how APIs work in many different contexts so you can better understand the context you will be using them in.

Crafting an API strategy is an art. We have offered the best advice we can about how we have seen this art practiced. More will be revealed as companies gain and share their experience. This book makes no claim to be exhaustive, but we hope that it turns out to be helpful. If we have done our job, you should now have a solid foundation to shape a strategy, understand how the API fits within your company, ask the right questions, identify the right resources, and more.

One warning: Don't look at a program for creating an API as a technical project. Keep one foot in the tech world and the other in the business world. Let the technology serve and influence the business direction, not dominate it. Listening to your developers (who are often technical by nature) will shape the program in ways you hadn't considered. But that should only happen within the framework of the overarching strategy.

An API is a tactic for implementing a business strategy, a tool for creating business value. Like any tactic, APIs have their own logic, their own personality. Now that you understand more about what APIs are and how they work, we hope that you find them as fascinating and transformational as we do.

About the Authors

Daniel Jacobson is Director of Engineering for the Netflix API, which is the primary distribution channel for getting movie and subscriber information to hundreds of Netflix-ready streaming devices. Prior to Netflix, Daniel led an engineering team at NPR where he created the NPR API as well as the content management system that drives NPR.org, mobile platforms, and all other digital presentations of NPR content.

As CTO of Apigee, **Greg Brail** has led the Apigee technology team as it deployed its API management technology for scores of customers. Prior to joining Apigee, Greg led the technology behind BEA's WebLogic JMS and Core Engine initiatives and developed the message-delivery infrastructure at TransactPlus. Greg spent his formative years with transaction-processing pioneer Transarc, where he deployed production systems at JPMorgan and elsewhere. He has held positions at Citibank and at IBM. Greg holds a degree in Computer Science from Brown University.

Dan Woods is a seasoned CTO, author, speaker, and entrepreneur with experience in business, computer science, journalism, and publishing. He is CTO and Editor of CITO Research, a firm dedicated to creating content to improve the performance of CIOs and CTOs. As an author, Dan has written or coauthored more than 20 books about business and technology, ranging from books about service-oriented architecture, open source, manufacturing, RFID, and wikis to the ideas driving the latest generation of enterprise applications, particularly in the face of Web 2.0's impact on the enterprise. Dan has written hundreds of white papers and conducted more than 1,000 interviews with experts in a variety of fields. He is also an invited speaker and moderator at international conferences. As a CTO, Dan built technology for companies ranging from Time Inc. New Media to TheStreet.com. He has managed the product development cycle from initial requirements through sales for websites and software products designed for the publishing and financial services industries. At TheStreet.com, his systems supported the company's successful IPO and handled millions of daily page views while the number of subscribers tripled and new lines of business were launched. At CapitalThinking, Dan's software was purchased by the IT departments of large financial institutions, including General Electric, JPMorgan Chase, and Citigroup. Dan holds an M.S. from Columbia University's Graduate School of Journalism and a B.A. in Computer Science from the University of Michigan. Since July 2008, Dan has been writing a column for Forbes.com.

The information you need, when and where you need it.

With Safari Books Online, you can:

Access the contents of thousands of technology and business books

- Quickly search over 7000 books and certification guides
- Download whole books or chapters in PDF format, at no extra cost, to print or read on the go
- Copy and paste code
- Save up to 35% on O'Reilly print books
- **New!** Access mobile-friendly books directly from cell phones and mobile devices

Stay up-to-date on emerging topics before the books are published

- Get on-demand access to evolving manuscripts.
- Interact directly with authors of upcoming books

Explore thousands of hours of video on technology and design topics

- Learn from expert video tutorials
- Watch and replay recorded conference sessions

Spreading the knowledge of innovators   safari.oreilly.com

Get even more for your money.

Join the O'Reilly Community, and register the O'Reilly books you own. It's free, and you'll get:

- $4.99 ebook upgrade offer
- 40% upgrade offer on O'Reilly print books
- Membership discounts on books and events
- Free lifetime updates to ebooks and videos
- Multiple ebook formats, DRM FREE
- Participation in the O'Reilly community
- Newsletters
- Account management
- 100% Satisfaction Guarantee

Signing up is easy:

1. **Go to: oreilly.com/go/register**
2. **Create an O'Reilly login.**
3. **Provide your address.**
4. **Register your books.**

Note: English-language books only

To order books online:
oreilly.com/store

For questions about products or an order:
orders@oreilly.com

To sign up to get topic-specific email announcements and/or news about upcoming books, conferences, special offers, and new technologies:
elists@oreilly.com

For technical questions about book content:
booktech@oreilly.com

To submit new book proposals to our editors:
proposals@oreilly.com

O'Reilly books are available in multiple DRM-free ebook formats. For more information:
oreilly.com/ebooks

O'REILLY®

Spreading the knowledge of innovators | oreilly.com